C000184519

FINDING FRANK

For you, Frank.
Then. Now. Forever.
♡ ♡ ♡

FINDING FRANK

BY RACHEL TOWNSEND

Cherish
EDITIONS

First published in Great Britain 2020 by Cherish Editions

Cherish Editions is a trading style of Shaw Callaghan Ltd & Shaw Callaghan 23 USA, INC.

The Foundation Centre

Navigation House, 48 Millgate, Newark

Nottinghamshire NG24 4TS UK

www.cherisheditions.com

Text Copyright © 2020 Rachel Townsend

British Library Cataloguing in Publication Data

A CIP catalogue record for this book is available upon request from the British Library

ISBN: 9781913615024

This book is also available in the following eBook formats:

ePUB: 9781913615031

Cover design by Bookollective

Typeset by Lapiz Digital Services Ltd

NOTE/DISCLAIMER

Cherish Editions encourages diversity and different viewpoints; however, all views, thoughts, and opinions expressed in this book are the author's own and are not necessarily representative of Cherish Editions as an organisation.

CONTENTS

INTRODUCTION

For as long as I can remember, I've wanted to write stories. Put words such as these together like carriages on a train. And here we are, you and I, meeting for the very first time. The hiss of brakes before my journey departs with you aboard, track and sleeper so familiar to me as we voyage back in time. Back to the beginning. A plume of steam rising high across a cloudless sky.

I was born in Cornwall in 1967, wedged firmly by birth between my younger brother Casper and my older sister Philippa. I suppose you could say I was the middle child, although my siblings and I also had two older half-brothers – Mike, our mother's son, and Ray, our father's son. Mike was always around when I was growing up. Ray wasn't.

Mike was born in Jamaica. He was born into a silent world. The shock of seeing his tiny frame, without any ears, and hearing his pitiful cry, must have been deeply distressing for my mother. His fate, however, was not to be pigeonholed by the unfortunate circumstances of his illegitimate birth, but by an evil drug, which was to become infamous for affecting so many children around the world. Many were born without arms or legs because of this inadequately tested drug, given to thousands of pregnant women to help them with morning sickness. Mike was branded a 'thalidomide' – a term that would be used to describe him from the day of his birth, as if he were some kind of object to be verbally abused.

Less than four years after Mike was born, my father would meet my mother in a Jamaican doctor's surgery. He had been in Jamaica for some time, on a posting from England, and after acquiring a small injury while playing his piano, he dropped into the surgery to have his finger examined.

My mother was a mixed-race Jamaican beauty – a real-life beauty queen – and my father was instantly captivated by her. Without hesitation, he asked her out. That very same evening, as they danced cheek to cheek, he proposed to her and within a few short months, they were married. As soon as my father had legally adopted Mike, the young family left Jamaica for a new posting on a small island in the Indian Ocean.

It must have been a difficult decision for my father, taking on another man's son, not least because of the additional support Mike would need as he grew up, profoundly deaf in one ear and with only partial hearing in the other. But they soon forged a bond of love, those two — a bond that can only be made between a father and son.

Throughout my childhood years, my father was employed by a large telecommunications company, which posted him to destinations all over the world, with us and the chaos of all our family in tow. In each new destination, another child was born. Before I was five years old, we had lived in England, Jamaica and Barbados. By now, there were four of us.

I first met Ray, my older half-brother, when I was nine years old. He was nineteen and had come to stay with us in Barbados for a few weeks. I only discovered several years later, that the reason for his visit was due to the untimely death of his mother. He had found her lifeless body one morning and an empty bottle of paracetamol tablets next to her bed. This gruesome discovery continued to affect him throughout his adult life. It didn't take much for him to turn to drink, where I believe he is still trying, mostly unsuccessfully, to drown out that devastating event, which forever changed his destiny, a destiny with so much unfulfilled potential. Tragically, his life was not the only one to be blighted by the premature death of a loved one, taken away by their own hand.

Growing up in Barbados provided me with a wonderfully rich and fertile soil for my keen young mind. I often yearn for the warmth of the people, the cool Atlantic sea breezes, the rhythmic calypso music and the sweet smell of the rum distilleries hiding in the tall sugarcane fields. It remains a part of me, not least because my mother, Casper and his family continue to live there.

Over the years, however, the rest of us have decanted, one by one, back to England: first Philippa, then me, then my father and lastly, Mike. I believe we all had one thing in common. We were desperate to get as far away as possible from my tyrant of a mother.

There, I've said it.

When I first decided to write this book, I wasn't sure whether I would be saying much about her at all. I wasn't sure whether I could be brave enough to be honest about what happened to us. I wanted to protect my siblings, who more than likely would feel the same weight of shame at the thought of our experiences becoming public. I also wanted to protect myself. I resolved then to write this book under a pseudonym, in the hope that it would provide us with a greater degree of anonymity.

I suppose, if you are reading this, the invisible hand that lays lightly on the lid of Pandora's Box is slowly releasing her grasp. But for now, at least, our family secret remains safely hidden in the depths of this developing manuscript of mine.

This is my story.

CHAPTER 1

My earliest memory of my mother was not of her violent
temper. It was, instead, of one of the very few times I
witnessed her genuine concern for me – although I would
not go as far as saying it was her love that I felt on that day,
many years ago, in our house in Jamaica.

In this first memory of my mother, I am three and we
have woken up to yet another power cut. I know this because
my fan has stopped and the house is quiet and humid. The
birdsong outside my window seems louder.

My father is boiling water in a small saucepan on the hob.
His shadowy morning cheeks prickle like a wire brush when
he kisses me good morning. I watch him dispense the steaming
water into a square, plastic ice cream container before he
carries it into the bathroom, with me trailing behind. He turns
on the cold tap, loud and full. Two cool drops bounce out of
the sink; one lands on my nose, the other on my eyelid. That
makes me laugh.

I love watching my father shave. The upward sweeps he
makes along his upstretched neck with his heavy metal razor.
Like roads through foam. Foam he whips up like meringue,
with a thick round brush. The brush has a wooden handle and
it lives inside a ceramic container. It rattles when I shake it.

The container is solid and white. Like heavy glass. I'm holding it with two hands. I have been told I must be careful *or it will break*. I press my nose into it. I like the smell. It smells like him. Safe. There is a flat, round bar of soap at the bottom of the container, dry and cracked, until my father adds a few drops of water and sets to work with his whipping brush.

The ice cream tub balances precariously on the side of the sink. It is softening rapidly, although I don't know that. I reach out to touch it. I poke at it. There is a faded blue picture of a swallow, with part of its wing missing, scratched off with age. The malleable container tips forward. Its scalding contents spill over onto my cheeks and naked chest.

The shock of it.

I gasp. A sharp intake of breath and I am falling backwards, onto the bathroom floor. Hard. My only protection, the pair of white shorts I am wearing. They have tiny strawberries embroidered on a single back pocket.

The pain begins. Like a jellyfish stuck fast to my face and chest. My skin begins to peel off. I am pulling at it.

My high-pitched screams bring my mother running in from outside, where she has been meticulously hanging out the washing in neat, orderly rows. Seeing her expression stops my wailing instantly. Like I'm a ragdoll, my mother manoeuvres my burning body swiftly into a sitting position on top of one of the kitchen worktops where I remain, stunned, as she rummages around in a nearby cupboard, desperate to find a bottle with odd-smelling white lotion. It smells like toilets. She lathers it liberally all over my face and chest. I begin to cry again as the pain rushes back into my body, this time with a vengeance.

'Tim, *what have you done?*' she screams at my father.

Through my tears and the stinging pain, I know that my father is not responsible. It was me who grabbed the container.

I emptied the entire contents of scalding water over myself.
Why is she screaming at him?

This is my very first memory of her.

I really don't remember much about my mother before
that, although my father always maintained that she was
gentle and sweet to each of us when we were babies — when
we were helpless and entirely dependent on her. Before we
developed our own minds.

We leave Jamaica two years later and head back to England.
But we don't stay long, because my mother hates the
cold weather.

In less than a year, we are on the move again, travelling to
Barbados on a very large and rusty banana boat called the
Geest Tide. I am standing on deck watching the huge swell
riding up the side of the ship before it retreats, far below me.
It's a long way down. The swell rolls and as it rises, it spits
salty spray at me. The towering, rusty walls of the ship loom
large behind me and only a thick railing separates me from a
vast expanse of ocean. I fall in love with the excitement of it.

Our first stop in Barbados is a south coast hotel. Once the
sun has set and night has drawn in, I stand outside in my bare
feet, listening to the sound of the tiny whistling frogs. I've
seen only one before, the colour of wet sand with two black
eyes. The grass is lush and damp between my toes. It feels like
plastic. Vivid blue and green spotlights shine up into the palm
trees and exotic plants. We live in one of the whitewashed
villas dotted at jaunty angles around the beautifully manicured
gardens. A new playground.

In no time at all, we are packing once again. My father has
found us a lovely coral stone house to rent. He works only a
few hundred yards away. Each morning, he waves us goodbye

and sets off with his leather briefcase, disappearing down the steep hill at the bottom of our garden, through a densely wooded path, which pops out onto a busy main road below. Directly opposite the path is my father's office. To me, it's a giant pink and orange skyscraper. In reality, it is probably only six or eight storeys high.

My siblings and I go to school, we fall over and scrape our knees, we learn to ride bikes and fly kites. Normal things like that. I have a pet tortoise called Touché. I like the way he eats bananas, with his long, wrinkled neck and pointy mouth, snapping at the soft fruit as if he were angry.

I grow taller. I am a skinny child. My skin is coffee-coloured from playing outside in the sun and my hair is a mess of golden-blonde curls. Perhaps my most prominent feature is my eyes. They are olive green with flecks of saffron around my pupils and a deep grey rim surrounding each iris. People often stare at my eyes. It makes me feel uncomfortable.

And all the while my mother is becoming more and more unhappy. And more and more angry. She shouts all the time. Mostly at my father.

I am almost five years old, playing quietly on my own in my bedroom with my brother's Fisher Price garage set. I can hear my mother's raised voice coming from somewhere across the house. She's shouting at my father. *Again.* My heart begins to beat a little faster. I feel the familiar rush of adrenaline shooting through my small frame.

I look around for somewhere to hide.

Her voice is growing louder. And closer. She's shouting at my brother now, outside in the corridor. Feet away. I can hear myself breathing. I jump to my feet. *Is anything untidy?* I am frantic. I tuck the nearside corner of my sheet in again. Tighter.

I smooth down the green spread on top of my bed, as she has shown me. So that there are no folds in it. It must be flat.

Moments later, she appears in my bedroom doorway. My heart jumps clean out of my chest. I want to run away, but I'm frozen to the spot. I pray silently that she will leave. My eyes sting. I dare not blink. She approaches me and draws her hand above her head. It pauses briefly. A single, defining moment. *Before.* She slaps me clean across my face. Hard. I am stunned. What have I done? I don't understand.

That is the first time. The first of many.

My father hopes a change might make my mother happy and so we move a few times over the next few years. But try as he may, he is never able to make anything right for her. And he really does try to do everything in his power to please her. Still, she remains angry. And she grows more and more violent.

We are now in our third rented home and I can hear my mother's raised voice coming from the kitchen. This is how it always starts. I stand, rooted to the spot, ears pricked, like a dog. And then my father's voice, soft and low. I can't make out what he's saying but I know his tone well enough. He is trying to placate her. He. Is. Wasting. His. Time. By now, I am almost eight, but already I know that one of us will be hit or something must be broken before she is spent ... before she is ready to retreat into the solitude of her darkened bedroom, like a hermit crab with its meal, slamming the bedroom door behind her.

I hear a loud *crack* as her hand connects with something.

'Carmen,' my father pleads. I hear *that.* She must have hit him hard. *Who will be next?* My heart is beating so fast I begin to feel faint. I am powerless to move. But this time, she doesn't come for me. Or anyone else. Everything is quiet. My body sags with relief. Very gradually, my heart begins to slow until I can no longer feel it hammering away inside my ribs. Thump. Thump. Thump. Fight. Flight. *Freeze.* Always, I freeze. I learned that from my father.

Later, we are all sitting around the dinner table in silence. Each one of us, not daring to look at the other. I steal a sideways glance at my father. His glasses are sitting oddly on his face. They are broken. My father has done his very best to mend them with masking tape wrapped around the nose piece, but he's made a terrible job of it. I sit there wanting to cry. But it won't do not to eat. My food is a tasteless texture inside my mouth.

My mother also likes to take her temper out on my father's radio, the one he keeps on his bedside table so he can listen to the BBC World Service wherever he happens to be in the world. It bears many scars of having been hurled onto the floor. It is taped up, like his glasses. There are some pieces missing. Despite this, the radio works. It brings my father comfort to hear a familiar English voice. My mother doesn't like that at all.

My father gets through a lot of radios over the years. And a lot of glasses.

Sometimes, when my father takes the blows, I am right there in the thick of it all as he cowers. He remains completely silent with both arms above his head as he stumbles backwards, away from her.

Often, she lashes out at him while he's driving. With all four of us sullen in the back seat.

'Let's go for a drive,' she will say, to no one in particular. *Dread.* I loathe these family outings most of all.

We're heading over to the east coast on the opposite side of the island. We pull out onto the main road and my mother's angry tirade begins almost immediately. We've been in the car for eight minutes. I know this because I've been counting. One to sixty. Eight times. My left fist is closed and my thumb and two fingers are neatly tucked into my right fist.

'Stop riding the white line!' she barks. Suddenly, I feel claustrophobic. *Hot.* Squashed into the back seat of the car with my three siblings. Our legs are stuck together in the heat. There is no escape.

Her hand lashes out, lightning quick, striking my father on the side of the face as he endeavours to steer our orange Fiat 128 in a *straight line*. The way my mother wants everything to be.

My father drives on. He is silent. Each one of us has a downturned mouth, frowning in the back. Looking straight ahead. At nothing.

CHAPTER 2

When I am ten, in a final attempt to please my mother, my
father decides to withdraw his retirement pension fund, a
substantial lump sum, and buy a plot of land to build us the
perfect family home.

The land is located in one of the most prestigious areas
of the island, on the edge of a beautiful and exclusive golf
course. It appeals to my mother. She is immediately caught up
with tiles, fabric and the best shape for a swimming pool. I am
deeply grateful to see her so distracted, but we are living in the
eye of a hurricane.

When the house is finally complete and the outside walls
are dirty with fresh red mud and young plants, my mother
invites her friends for dinner parties or for a swim in the pool.
Fake smiles and dead eyes behind huge sunglasses. (The pool
is kidney-shaped in the end.)

But when we are alone again, she rages on and on. Nothing
is ever good enough. *Nothing.* Our house has a Spanish name,
one that means "*joy*". However, that was as far away from the
truth as it could possibly be.

I'm woken up at some ungodly hour of the night by the
sound of pots and pans being smashed around in the

kitchen. Our newly-built house is designed around a large courtyard filled with lush tropical plants. The bedroom doors and adjacent kitchen, with its wooden louvred windows, open out onto the courtyard. Any sound, therefore, carries easily across the house.

My heart begins to beat very fast whenever I hear those pans. I feel sure it will jump clean out of my chest one day. I lie in bed, terrified. My eyes wide like an aye-aye. I know what's coming; my mother is in yet another one of her rages and *how dare* anyone be sleeping while she is boiling over with anger.

It's a little after five and early enough that not even the birds have begun to sing. Any minute now, she will come crashing into my bedroom.

The door is flung open and I jump to my feet, like a soldier. She begins hauling open my drawers, one at a time. She pulls *all* of my clothes out and throws them onto the floor. A pile of clean laundry. At least the floor is clean. You could stick your gum on it and put it right back in your mouth. With no bits.

'What do you call this, Rachel?' she shrieks. 'Do you think these are folded properly?'

One by one, she makes me pick my clothes up off the floor. She is standing over me. Close enough to strike. T-shirts first. I fold them in half, lengthways, with the sleeves matching each other precisely, and then I fold them once again, bottom to top. Next, I fold my shorts in half, widthways. These are much easier.

My efforts are not to her liking. She pulls the last item out again and throws it back onto the floor. Then she hits me clean across the face with the back of her hand. *Crack.* Her bony knuckles connect with my cheek. Mostly, it's the back of her hand that comes flying out, still wet from washing in the kitchen for the millionth time. I try again to do what she's asked of me. It's difficult because my hands are trembling with the adrenaline coursing through my body. It's like fire inside my veins. My face is hot with indignation. There is a huge lump, permanently lodged inside my throat. Like a walnut. I hate her so utterly. With every single fibre of my being. But I won't cry. I haven't cried in years.

Not long after my tenth birthday, I hear my mother as she begins to work herself up again. Nothing unusual here. She is shouting at my father. Like a radar, with pinpoint accuracy, I follow the sound of her voice as she moves into the living room to find her next victim. This time it's my sister Philippa.

'Look at the tassels, *Phil-i-ppa*,' she cries, like machine-gun fire. 'You're sitting in here doing nothing when you can see that they are *all over the place*!'

I hear a chair scraping and something unintelligible. Philippa will now be kneeling on the floor, straightening out the tassels on the living room rug. She will be brushing them out with her small hands. Perfectly straight. Or else.

My mother moves out into the courtyard. She walks down the corridor into my half-brother's room. More shouting. Hurried apologies, over and over, from Mike.

'Sorry, Mum. *Soreeee*!' His voice breaks. I wonder what he's done? Mike is good. He is compliant. Right then, something inside of me snaps. Like a fluorescent glow stick. It washes down from the top of my head to the tip of my toes. I am standing upright in my bedroom. Next in line. My mother storms in. Fire and brimstone. *That frown.* Meets granite.

'Take the hair *out of your brush*!' She points at my dressing table.

'No,' I reply, flatly. With dead eyes. My very first refusal.

She erupts. Spewing lava. The back of her ring-knuckled fingers meets the side of my face with a loud *crack*. I do not flinch. Cold. Hatred.

'Do. It. Again,' I seethe. Glaring. Daring her.

Like lightning, her hand connects with my cheek once again. It stings like mad but I don't flinch. Not once.

'And *again*,' I hiss.

This time, she just looks at me strangely. As if she has no idea where she is. She is sleepwalking. Her raised hand crumples like paper and she drops it loosely to her side. The strength is returning to my legs. This is new. I turn and run. Past her. Outside into the garden.

I am running towards the gate but something stops me dead in my tracks. Two hundred yards away on the golf course, next to the fourteenth tee, my father is sitting on a bench. Shoulders hunched over. Like a dead tulip. He has abandoned us. *What a coward!*

From then on, whenever my mother tries to hit me, I make a valiant attempt at grabbing her arm/the hairbrush/the rolling pin to prevent her from hurting me. Physically.

One day, I will get away from you.
Far, far away.

My wish is granted when I am eleven.

My siblings and I are all summoned together into our pristine sitting room. My mother speaks first.

'Your father has received a new posting to the Middle East and we have both decided that it is best for all you children to go to boarding school in England. You will start in September, after the summer holidays, and after that, you will be spending the school holidays in Bahrain.'

I dart a quick look at Philippa, instantly recognising the glint in her eye. My heart flips with excitement.

The best news is yet to come.

'I, however, am going to stay here in Barbados,' she continues, in her rather forced, haughty voice, 'because I will not be able to tolerate the heat in Bahrain.'

My heart begins to sing! This is the *best* news of my life. Perhaps most young children would be horrified at being told they were going to be sent thousands of miles away from their home, but me? Absolutely *not*! I feel as if I am being sent away to Disneyland. Finally, *finally*, I will get away from her.

For the first time in my young life, I will be rid of my mother. I am ecstatic.

The business is a B... continue...

I, however, often right to any kind in Barbados. The
continues in her rather bland, naughty verse, because I will
not be able to replace the hen to Barbados...

Ah, how I been cheated! Here is the bad news, in short.
Perhaps people would rather would be horrified at being told
that was a joke... here are thousands of miles away from Phila-
an orange...? Anyway, such and I and as I am being carried
to Denteland. Finally, finally, I will get to my front line
for the first time in my bones that I will be led as in my
mother, I am certain.

CHAPTER 3

On the very first day of lessons, we all gather in classroom 1A – daygirls and boarders alike. Each one of us is given a selection of new exercise books for the coming year. One of the exercise books is an orange rough book. It's been issued for us to write our notes or to doodle in, but mostly it's to encourage us to write on something other than our desks.

We've each been allocated a wooden desk, with an inkwell that we will never use. They have open-top lids and are decorated with the obligatory graffiti of bored children, long since left. I soon discover a piece of hardened chewing gum stuck fast to the underside of my desk and I catch myself absent-mindedly picking away at it. Not pleasant but addictive. Like a scab.

A blond-haired girl is watching me as I carefully draw a horse's head on the front of my rough book. I vaguely become aware of her presence and I look up to find her standing next to my desk. She is strikingly pretty, with clear blue eyes and a mischievous grin.

'Will you draw one for me?' she asks confidently, cocking her head on one side. I smile and nod back at her. I am happy to oblige.

'I'm Penny, by the way,' she says, handing over her book.

'Rachel,' I reply, as I take the book from her and put mine to one side. I open the orange cover and I press it flat at the seam. Ready to fulfil her request.

A firm friendship is forged from that very moment... a friendship that will last over thirty-five years but will come to an end in jealousy and mistrust.

Bahrain is unlike anything I have ever experienced before. The landscape is dry and barren, dotted with date palms and neat, man-made highways, which cut through the desert, joining the outlying villages with the main town of Manama.

This is the first time I've seen people hidden away under black and white robes. Or *not* seen them. Curiously, the men wear white and the women wear black. They float through the villages followed by their children who, unlike them, are dressed in shorts or jeans and brightly coloured t-shirts, with their thick, dark hair uncovered, too young for the demands of their religion.

My family has been given a three-bedroomed, box-shaped bungalow near Saar village, on a compound specifically for European expatriates. There are several other houses in the compound, each painted white, with flat roofs and central air-conditioning to keep the air cool inside. There is a pool at the end of our compound where we can swim when the sun is low enough in the sky to make the heat more tolerable.

My father takes us to the souk in Manama, appropriately dressed, with our arms and legs covered. We step into a different world, vibrant and exciting. Dates clinging to their branches, piled high and shrivelled in the hot sun. Exotic perfumes, like honey in carved glass bottles, arranged in neat rows, tinkling against each other. The strong smell of the polish used to buff the many brass coffee pots and figurines.

Shouts in a language strange and harsh, accompanied by smiling eyes and thick moustaches.

My father, no longer stifled by my mother's toxic, overbearing presence, endeavours to make up for all of his previous shortcomings. And, for the very first time, I experience what it feels like to be truly free — ironic, in a country where freedom is not synonymous with the culture, certainly less so for women and girls.

As my father is at work all day, he thinks it's a good idea to organise membership for each of us at the Dilmun Club. Quite literally, it's an oasis for expatriates. It has an outdoor swimming pool, tennis courts, squash courts, an indoor pool table and a dart board. We have all the entertainment we could ever wish for while my father is out at work.

I make friends easily with others who, like me, are home for the holidays, having travelled back from various schools all over England. Our parents are similarly attracted by the fat wage packets and tax-free salaries of the Gulf. We are left to our own devices from morning until late in the afternoon. It becomes the bedrock of my teenage years.

It is here that I meet Frank.

I am a little restless. A few of the girls have gone outside for a swim, but I'm not in the mood to get changed and then get wet and dry myself off, and get dressed all over again.

I look over at the pool table and decide to play a game. I walk to the dusty chalkboard and write my initials on it with a miniscule piece of blue chalk. The only piece I can find sitting on the top of the board. After I've written on the board, I turn away and find an empty table nearby. I wait my turn. My fingers are blue.

The rules in the club are "winner stays on" and, without a doubt, Frank is one of the best pool players in the club. He is also fiercely competitive. As you might expect, he is pretty much a permanent fixture on the pool table. When it's my turn to play, he comes looking for me.

'Rachel?' he enquires, rather shyly. I'm distracted by the others outside in the swimming pool. I'm wondering if I should have joined them. I look at Frank and something rather odd happens to my insides. Like I've eaten spicy food. I *see* him, as if for the very first time. His enormous brown eyes, soft and kind. His freshly washed hair, shiny like a polished conker. He's wearing a string of leather around his neck with a dark green malachite cross pendant. It hangs down just below his prominent Adam's apple, which moves when he talks. I take a deep breath and swallow hard. My mouth is suddenly dry and my voice cracks when I attempt to reply. 'Y– yes, am I up?' I clear my throat and smile back at him, nervously. *How have I never noticed him before?* Frank turns away and walks back to the pool table. I follow behind, taking in the scent of his shampoo. Fresh and clean, as if he's just stepped out of the shower. I notice his hair is a little longer at the back, just reaching the nape of his neck. It curls very slightly at the ends. My heart begins to beat a little faster. I drop my gaze to his broad shoulders and narrow hips. He's earned the nickname Snake Hips. Some of the girls were using it earlier, giggling in a way that only teenage girls can giggle. Suddenly, I know why. When he walks, it's mesmerising. *Sexy*.

'*Shit,*' I mutter under my breath. Frank is affecting me more than I like. I feel a little out of control. This feeling is completely new to me. Unsettling. And exciting.

The game passes in a blur of steely determination on my part to hide my jangling nerves, coupled with an overwhelming urge to lose, so I can get away and take stock of whatever the hell has taken over my insides. I needn't have worried. It doesn't take long for Frank to sink the black ball. It clatters noisily into the pocket and rolls out of sight. I hear a sharp *clack* as it joins the other balls inside the table.

He looks over at me, leaning on his cue with a smug grin on his face as he slowly raises a defiant eyebrow. *Infuriating.* In return, I adopt a rather haughty attitude towards defeat. Much safer than revealing the turmoil of being so close to him.

I begin to look forward to my trips to the Dilmun Club even more after that.

Everyone at the club gels together to form one large tight-knit group. There are around thirty of us. Some, like me, make the numbers up with brothers and sisters.

My father drops us off at the club early, on his way to work. My half-brother, Mike; my sister, Philippa; my younger brother, Casper; and me. As Mike is the oldest, my father asks him to keep an eye on the rest of us. He says this every time we climb out of his huge air-conditioned Pontiac.

We are the first to arrive.

I find a table and put my bag down on it. It's close to the pool table but not *too* close. And now the waiting game begins. I sit down and look back towards the door. Each and every time someone walks in, I'm hoping it will be Frank. And every time it isn't, my heart sinks like a stone. Frank often arrives an hour after me. Sometimes more. *This is torture.* And then, there he is. My heart flips. Twice.

I immediately pretend to be fully occupied, fumbling around inside my bag for nothing in particular. Totally ignoring Frank and yet completely aware of him. I see the top half of him as he walks past me. In my peripheral vision. A flash of khaki. A sleeve. Fingers.

Once my nerves settle down, I walk over to the pool table and chalk up my initials on the board, *R. T.* Wobbly letters in white. I return to my seat. Quickly.

Frank is lining up a shot. I'm directly in his eyeline. He looks up from the cue ball. Our eyes meet, briefly. A jolt of electricity shoots through my entire body. *Breathless*. I look away as casually as I can, as if this is only a chance exchange. I remember that Frank was in my dream last night.

He is seeping into me.

Pedro, a good friend of Frank's, sits down next to me. I'm totally absorbed in the game of pool being played in front of me and I only realise someone is there when I feel the bench depress. Frank is playing my brother, Casper. He's beating him ruthlessly. Pedro nods at Frank. An acknowledgment of some sort. Casper is upset. He hates losing.

'Rach, Frank and I are going to meet some of the others tonight at the Holiday Inn in Manama. They've got live music in the bar from six to nine. Fancy joining us?' Pedro asks with a smile. *Does he know?* I accept immediately.

Pedro, Frank and I file past a life-size ice carving of a swan and then we disappear into the subdued lighting of the bar. Purple and gold. Pedro is not a good time-keeper and tonight, we are the last to arrive. The bar is full. Buzzing. The air is thick with aftershave and the smell of Marlborough Lights. Pedro walks off to find the toilet. Frank and I sit down on one of the brightly coloured velvet chairs.

Under the spotlights, perched high up on their stools at the front of the room, Babs and Mary have already begun taking requests. They know them all.

Everyone begins to sing it. We belt out at the top of our lungs. Laughing. And me sitting close enough to Frank to feel the heat of his thigh. Stealing glances at him.

Frank looks down at my empty glass. 'Drink, Rach?'

'Yes, thanks. Pepsi, please.' I reply, rather shyly. We rarely drink alcohol. Not in those days, at least. I don't like the taste. But sometimes it is unavoidable.

'Anyone having a birthday *to*-day?' Babs shouts out to the crowd.

'Me!' a voice pipes up. Whether it's true or not, Mary winks at the barman. It's a signal to send over an exotic-looking cocktail, complete with paper umbrella, and a cocktail stick holding pineapple chunks and Maraschino cherries, squished together. Sweet and juicy. I like those bits, perched on the top of a tequila sunrise or a piña colada.

During the Easter holidays, a few months after my sixteenth birthday, the Dilmun Club organises a dhow boat trip for the entire group. It's a welcome change from the cool and relatively dark interiors of the club and the Holiday Inn.

We meet in the bright warm sunshine, down at the dock in Manama. It's early and we are waiting for permission to board the large wooden dhow, which is anchored and bobbing gently in the water next to us. The sleek wooden hull of a bygone era.

One by one, we stumble aboard, thin arms weighed down with ice boxes, rucksacks and bottles of water. I find a place to put down my things. I'm feeling self-conscious in my new surroundings, and excited.

There are shouts in Arabic behind me. Heavy ropes are pulled and tied and sails billow open. A huge triangle of salty linen above my head. Flapping and snapping in the wind. Filling up. I hold on as we bob to starboard and begin to pick up speed. Moss green water turns to velvet blue. On course to a sandbank far out in the warm waters of the Arabian Gulf.

I copy the others and take off my t-shirt. My young breasts are full and pert in my bright red bikini top, like two torpedoes. They bounce slightly as I shift my weight from the balls of my feet onto my heels, trying to stay balanced as I take off my shorts. I turn my face into the wind, close my eyes for a moment and breathe the salty air deep into my lungs. The warmth of the sun on my bare skin. The sea surrounding me. *This*. I love this feeling.

I've grown taller over the past year. I don't want to be tall. I don't like being noticed. My once golden-blonde hair is now much darker. It's almost the same colour as Frank's – a rich chestnut brown – with tight corkscrew curls. It's impossible to tame and has a life of its own. It flicks into my eyes and blows across my face. Irritated, I tuck it behind my ears.

We finally drop anchor in the still wind, with the hot sun high in the sky. Sweat and suntan lotion. The sails are rolled away. We wait to cool off in the sea below, our eyes trained on the skipper. My hands grip the edge of the boat. I am eager.

With a sweep of his hand, we leap in like water bombs. Shrieks and splashes. With masks, snorkels and flippers, our ocean adornments. Laughter.

Almost immediately, someone spots a small group of dolphins. I am treading water. I pull my mask over my face. Excited. Gasping. I kick my legs out. I'm trying to keep my head above the surface. The water is warm. Salty. The dolphins are a few feet away from me, under the boat. My eyes open wide. This is the closest I've ever been to a dolphin. I am mesmerised by their grace. Grey and white shadows. Lightning quick. Twisting and dancing around each other. Cautiously, I swim a little closer. I am a strong swimmer but I don't know what to expect. They are large and many. But they keep their distance, cutting through the surface above me before diving back, in a whirlpool of tiny white bubbles. With a strong flick of their tails, they are gone.

Reluctantly, we return to the boat, beads of salty water on our skin. Breathless with excitement. I am hungry. I pat myself dry and sit down on the hot wooden deck to eat my lunch. Frank is a few feet away from me. He is standing. If I reached out, I could touch his naked calf, round like an orange. But I don't.

We set sail once more, heading back towards the mainland. Quiet now. Sobered by our swim and a belly full of food. The sails billow out on the wind, driving us forward. The salty spray is now a powdery dust on my shoulders. I stick my tongue out and taste it. I look around. Everyone is either sitting or lying on the deck on a patchwork of brightly coloured towels. Except Frank. Frank is leaning with both hands on the side of the boat. Big and strong. I can see the fine blond hairs on the back of his fingers. *I'm that close.* I watch those hands whenever we play pool together. I imagine how they might feel if he touched me. Their heat on my body.

He's wearing a floppy cricket hat, but it's his very small speedos that catch my attention. Red, blue and white. A swirly pattern. They leave little to the imagination. I can see his bulge straining against the fabric. Frank doesn't have one ounce of fat on him. He is all sinew and limb, like the trunk of a Divi-divi tree. And broad. He seems lost in the expanse of sea as it rolls away from the dhow, trailing froth and foam in our wake, white against velvet. I want to kiss him. His salty mouth.

His stomach twitches.

'I'm in love with you, Frank,' I whisper. Only my mind hears it. The inside part of my skull. If only the wind would carry my words. A gentle breath. *Does he know?* Probably not. I frown. My furrowed brow is shiny with sweat. I need to work harder. Make him notice me. I take out my sunscreen and very slowly, I begin to apply it, in a manner I hope will catch his attention.

Frank becomes my entire world.

As for my mother, for almost two years, I hardly think about her. Not until my father, in a moment of utter madness, begs her to join us in Bahrain to see if they can repair their marriage.

My heart sinks to the floor when I see her at Heathrow Airport at the end of school term. She looks beautiful, smiling and happy to see us all after so long. But I am left cold and unmoved.

It doesn't take much time at all for the same angry monster to emerge. And as for the heat in Bahrain, well, that was never the reason why my mother stayed behind in Barbados. I soon discover that she'd been having an affair. My miserable, angry mother. Who would have believed *that*? And the reason we were all shipped off to boarding school was so she could carry on seeing her lover.

My mother's arrival soon puts a stop to much of our freedom and enjoyment. We are now expected to go on family outings together, where her anger is never very far from the surface.

We are sitting in the living room together one evening, Mike, Philippa and I, when the phone rings on the nearby coffee table. Philippa leans over, picks up the cream plastic handset and speaks into the mouthpiece.

'Philippa speaking, may I help you?'

'A young lady for you,' Philippa says to Mike, with a gleam in her eye. He gets up to take the call in my parents' bedroom where there is a second handset and a little more privacy. I notice a smile playing around the corners of his mouth as he leaves the room. As soon as we hear Mike's disjointed voice amplified through the handset in Philippa's hand, she replaces it. The thick spiral plastic chord between the handset and the phone has twisted tightly around itself. It sticks out at a jaunty angle. *My mother won't like that,* I think to myself absent-mindedly. She often stops to untangle the chord by untwisting it until the handset sits neatly again in the cradle on top of the phone.

As if on cue, my mother appears from the kitchen. She walks straight over to the phone and immediately picks up the handset. I've seen her do this literally a thousand times. Only this time, she puts the phone to her ear. I can hear Mike talking, although his voice is muffled. I'm shocked. I look over to Philippa, whose expression has suddenly turned to thunder. My mother is blatantly eavesdropping on Mike's conversation. Her eyes dart from each of our faces, neither caring nor registering our obvious surprise and disapproval. I've never seen Philippa looking quite so angry. She leans over and snatches the phone out of my mother's hand. She places it gently back in its cradle and she stands up. It's my mother's turn to look shocked.

This is an act of defiance.

I've never seen Philippa defy my mother and suddenly, I'm frightened. I can feel the adrenaline rushing through my body and I want to run.

'What *the hell* do you think you are doing, girl?' my mother hisses with fury.

'What the hell do *you* think you're doing, Mum? Mike is having a private conversation!' Philippa shouts back, pointing to the phone.

Shit. Right then, all hell breaks loose.

My mother runs out of the room and into the kitchen. She storms back in with a pair of scissors as Philippa is escaping into the hallway. My mother is right behind her, holding the scissors in front of her with murderous intent. I jump to my feet, terrified, but my legs are like jelly and I almost collapse back onto the sofa. *She's going to kill her, she's going to kill her*, I scream inside my head but I'm much too frightened to speak. My words are gone. I stumble out into the hallway just in time to see Philippa with her back against the wall and my mother holding the scissors up against her throat.

'*How dare you!*' she seethes between gritted teeth, 'How dare you tell me how to conduct myself! Just remember this, *girl*. I gave you life and I will take it away!' She jabs the air with the scissors, menacingly, only inches away from Philippa's throat. I am powerless. I want to run forward and grab my mother's hair, great handfuls of it, and pull her backwards off her feet. I want to rip the scissors out of her hand. I want to protect my sister but I'm frozen. I can't move. Philippa is now sweating profusely. Her forehead is shiny and there are tiny beads of sweat dotted across her top lip. She looks scared. Unsure what to do next.

Just then, Mike appears in my parents' doorway. 'What are you doing, Mum?' he says, stunned. My mother immediately steps back, dropping her hand to her side with an expression I don't recognise. She briefly throws my sister a look before storming into the kitchen. Moments later, the utensil drawer slams shut.

Philippa looks at me blankly and walks slowly to our bedroom. Without saying a word, she closes the door behind her.

I often think about this encounter – the image of my mother holding a pair of scissors to my sister's throat – wondering what might have happened if Mike hadn't appeared when he did. And then I immediately try to forget.

Days later, my mother has confined us to our bedrooms and she has gone for a nap. We are not allowed out to see our friends at the club or in our street. There is no reason for this. We are being punished because she is angry. We are also bored, but I have an idea.

'Let's play Monopoly,' I say to Philippa. We find the box at the back of a cupboard with its torn corners and we both attempt to set up the game. Almost immediately, it becomes apparent that there are no dice in the box.

'Bugger,' I say.

I get up and open our bedroom door, slowly. It's quiet in the hall and I tiptoe over to Casper's room and creep in.

Casper is lying on his stomach on the bed, kicking his feet up and down and flicking through the pages of an old Guinness Book of Records. He looks up at me.

'Casper, can you sneak over to the Watsons' and borrow some dice so Philippa and I can play Monopoly? *Please*,' I add, clasping my hands together. He looks up at me and cocks his head to one side.

'Mum asleep?'

'Yep, but hurry, will you?' I whisper.

'Ok,' he says, slamming the book shut and swinging his legs down to the floor. Casper pretty much does what he's told and moments later he's sneaked down the hallway into the kitchen and left the house out of the back door. I return to my bedroom and linger in the doorway, peeking through a small crack between the door and the frame. I look back and whisper to Philippa. I tell her that Casper has gone across the road for some dice. My heart is pounding and I'm now beginning to feel quite anxious.

Suddenly, my mother's bedroom door opens and my mother steps out into the hallway. Her face is still crumpled with sleep. Shit, shit, *shit*.

She walks straight to the kitchen and immediately I know that Casper is going to be caught. There are no two ways about it. Right then I can hear my mother's shrill voice,

'Where the hell have you been, Casper? Did you go *out*?' She is shouting. I can't make out Casper's reply but, quick as a flash, he runs towards me, pulls open the door a few inches and throws the dice into our bedroom before running back into his. I close the door and retreat into the bedroom, scooping up the dice before sitting down heavily on my bed, cross-legged. I push the dice under my right buttock and look over to Philippa, who is biting her bottom lip. This won't end well for Casper.

Seconds later, I hear a loud crack where my mother has hit Casper. He cries out immediately but the beating doesn't end there. In between strikes, she is shouting. *Crazed*.

'Don't you e-ver disobey me, do you hear? *E-ver*!' And with one final slap, I hear Casper's door slam shut. I am grateful that she doesn't appear in our room but I'm feeling terrible for Casper, who I can hear whimpering through the walls. And guilty.

'I fucking hate her,' I hiss, to no one in particular. And I do. *Utterly*.

My mother never finds out about the dice and I'm eternally grateful to Casper for saying nothing. Now, at least, Philippa and I have something to do, but I don't much feel like playing a game.

That evening, before bed, we are talking in whispers to each other. We've been confined to our room for most of the day and have only been allowed out of our bedroom to eat. We still have no idea why. This is not at all unusual but over the years, we've learned how to entertain ourselves well enough.

I creep out of bed and crawl along the floor in the dark before pouncing onto Philippa's feet, which frightens the life out of her. She shrieks as I throw myself back onto my own bed, laughing loudly. She laughs too and it isn't very long before my mother flings open our door and switches on the light.

'I don't want to hear one more peep out of either of you!' she shouts, her face contorted with rage. Our smiles freeze on our faces, leaving our eyes cold. I am clutching the blanket tightly under my chin and I dare not breathe. My mother slams the door so hard that the dust in the air-conditioning unit above floats down onto the floor and onto Philippa's bed. The light is still on and Philippa looks over to me. Suddenly this is extremely funny and we struggle to suppress our laughter. It just won't do to be laughing while my mother is so angry. A bit like trying to stifle the giggles when you're meant to be quiet in assembly at school. We laugh under the covers, with our hands over our mouths, tears streaming down our faces at the ridiculousness of it all. *Hysterics*. But really, it's not funny at all.

Our only respite is when the holidays are over and it's time for us to return to London, and on to our various schools all over England. I miss Bahrain and my Dilmun Club friends, but I'm relieved to be leaving my mother behind. I miss Frank the most. I hate leaving him.

I only wish he felt the same.

CHAPTER 4

Back at boarding school in England, Penny provides me
with a second family who indoctrinate me into the quirky
and quintessentially English way of modern, pseudo-
aristocratic life. It's a stark contrast to my very strict, West
Indian upbringing. I am *horrified* at the way Penny speaks to
her parents.

'Fuck off, Daddy!' she shrieks. Her father is attempting to
move her chair so he can manoeuvre his big belly past her
at the kitchen table. Their house is huge, but the kitchen is
small in comparison, and the table in the centre of the room
takes up most of the space. Penny's father just grumbles a
little as he squeezes through the narrow gap behind her. But
nothing more is said. Wide-eyed, I look from one to the other,
but neither seems in any way fazed by the exchange. Penny is
buttering her toast and humming to herself. I soon learn this is
a perfectly normal way for them to interact with each other.

The following weekend, we drive down to Burwash for
afternoon tea, just the four of us. I love these trips with
Penny's parents. Penny and I in the back of their Land Rover
Defender. The metal seats have no cushions and Penny and
I rattle around, holding on. It's loud and we all shout at each
other to be heard.

We enter the tea shop and sit down at a round wooden table near the window. Penny's father orders. The young waitress, with her flowery dress and clean white apron, returns with a tray of silver pots. There is cream, strawberry jam and a plate of warm scones. They smell like sweet bread. There are two silver teapots, a silver jug of milk and a small silver sugar bowl. The sugar is white. I like white sugar. In Barbados the sugar was always brown. All the silver pots are slightly scratched on the outside. Penny's mother pours the tea. I watch the steam rise as my white china cup fills with golden liquid. I add milk and two teaspoons of sugar. It isn't much, as the silver teaspoon is only small. It's made in the shape of half an acorn. We build our scones. I put jam on mine first. Already, Penny wants more clotted cream.

'Mummy, order some more cream please. This pot is finished.'

'No, Penny, you've had quite enough already.' Her mother is pointing at Penny's plate, indicating the cream piled high on top of both halves of her scone. Despite everyone sitting around us, Penny screams a high, piercing scream. My mouth drops open. Wide.

'I want more cream! There isn't *nearly* enough,' she yells. The people around us are now looking over, stunned, like me. Penny's mother immediately gives in as she does every single time.

I soon learn that Penny often screams at the top of her lungs if she's told 'no.' I find her behaviour, especially when we are out, truly shocking. She loves to misbehave, and I love her.

Penny is a breath of fresh air and the perfect antidote for my long-suffering, stifled soul. She can do whatever she wants or say *anything*, it seems, without the fear of violent recrimination. This gives me an entirely different and liberating perspective on the world — and a vital life lesson.

At the same time, I share everything I have been taught about acceptable behaviour, and as a result, Penny's manners improve considerably.

'Penny, you *can't* say that,' I hiss at her when she calls her father 'a fat old lump' at the top of her voice, during dinner in a Kensington restaurant. He is trying to order another basket of bread. She just laughs.

'Penny, you *mustn't* do that,' I shout. We are both in the park and she is attempting to release the branch of a tree. She has bent the branch all the way down to the ground and there is an unsuspecting tabby cat still sitting on it. Thankfully, the cat steps off in the nick of time and walks away, oblivious. She has no intention of catapulting the cat but every intention of getting a reaction out of me. Penny thinks it's hilarious. Her blue eyes sparkle with mischief.

Over the next few years, Penny provides me with a very welcome escape from school. Almost every weekend, her parents invite me to stay, as a result of their daughter's "much improved behaviour" and her generally calmer demeanour. This suits Penny and me perfectly. We always have a fantastic time together.

I make a few very good friends at school. There is Robyn, also a day girl like Penny, and Molly – or Mo, as we like to call her – who is a boarder, like me. We find some respite from the monotony of school life by smoking up in the bushes on the school grounds whenever we have the opportunity to do so. Penny comes along with us although she doesn't smoke. I think she just likes the fact that we are all being naughty.

During my final year at school, everything at home changes. Again. My mother manages to persuade my father to take an early retirement option, after thirty-five years with his company, and return with her to Barbados. It's probably the worst decision of his life.

I have to say goodbye to my Dilmun Club friends and the freedom I've come to expect. I am heartbroken. For the very first time in my life, I've experienced the first stirrings of love, and I am gutted that nothing has developed between Frank and me. Soon, we will be leaving Bahrain for good. *How on earth will I say goodbye?* I can't bear the thought. Worse still, Frank only seems to see me as a friend. He's never once given me any indication he feels anything more. *Will he miss me?*

All too soon, it's my final night in Bahrain and I'm utterly miserable. Frank has promised to come over and say goodbye. I wait anxiously, looking out of the window of our sitting room at the road outside literally every two minutes, with my stomach in knots.

And then, there he is, *finally*, pulling up in his mother's yellow Honda Accord. I watch him stroll up to the front door and, despite knowing he's here, the noise of the doorbell makes me jump. I walk over on unsteady legs and let him into the cool air inside the house. I daren't speak as he follows me back into the sitting room. We are alone. Everyone else is packing. I feel like crying.

'All packed?' Frank asks cheerfully. A little *too* cheerfully. He sits down on the sofa. *Why is he so happy when I'm dying inside?* I desperately want him to pull me into his arms and kiss me deeply. I've been wishing it for *two whole summers*.

Instead, I force a smile. 'Yes, I finished packing yesterday. All except my toothbrush and washbag,' I reply, as casually as I can.

Really, Rach? Is that your best shot?

We make ridiculous small talk for a few more minutes before my father strides into the room, saying a swift hello and goodbye to Frank, indicating that it's time for him to leave. I stand up and follow Frank outside into the humid air, and I walk out to the car with him. My hopes of a final kiss are fading faster with each footstep. There's a lump forming inside my throat. I try and smile but I can't. The car door slams and then he is gone.

Just like that.

I'm devastated. I watch the red tail lights of his car retreating into the distance.

A hot tear slips down my cheek.

CHAPTER 5

I return to school feeling thoroughly depressed. Penny and Mo have now left and I no longer have anyone to hang around with. Several long-distance telephone calls follow, with me in tears, begging my father to let me leave. Finally, he consents, but only after I agree to retake my O-Levels, as I've managed to fail most of them the first time around.

But it isn't all bad. In the weeks that follow, something happens to buoy my dampened spirits. I receive a letter from Frank!

I wait until I'm back in my room before opening it with nervous fingers, savouring the delicious feeling that has spread throughout my body. I miss Frank deeply. Not a day goes by without me thinking about him.

I open the envelope carefully and pull out a letter, a few photographs and something small wrapped up in white tissue paper. First, I look at the photographs. One of them is a picture Frank has taken of a rock face during his holiday in Cyprus. On closer inspection, the photograph reveals two names, which Frank has carved into the rock.

Frank 4 Rachel.

I can't believe it. My jaw drops to the floor as my heart begins to soar. I unfold the letter and devour its contents.

Dear Rachel,

I'm back in Bahrain again after my holiday in Cyprus with Mum and Steve.

I was doing a lot of windsurfing and I found this place at the end of the beach with a cave. Have a look and see what I scratched in the rock. The other photos are of me windsurfing. I'm getting quite good now!

Rach, I was really sad when you left. I can't tell you how much. I really miss you! I've been meaning to tell you for so long how much I think of you but as you have probably guessed, I am a very shy guy! I hope you don't think badly of me, saying all this now. I just want you to know how I feel.

I have sent you a little present to remind you of me. I hope you like it! Maybe one day we will see each other again. I really hope we will.

Frank x

I read the letter again and again. Large, salty tears roll down my face.

Frank loves me!

I put the letter aside and carefully open the small package. Inside the tissue paper, I find Frank's malachite cross pendant. I close my fingers over it and hold it against my chest. My heart aches. The joy I feel is tinged with sadness at the futility of our situation. I'm stuck in boarding school and Frank is in Bahrain. It seems hopeless. And frustrating.

Frank's letter keeps me going for a long time, but not long after receiving it, I make the difficult decision not to reply. *What is the point in prolonging the heartache?*

I draw a line under it.

Frank's letter is an ending to our love; a love which never really had the chance to become anything real.

I often take the malachite pendant out and look at it with longing. I think - *what if?* But it only makes me feel worse, and so very soon I stop doing that altogether and I leave it in the back of my wooden jewellery box to become a memory.

This is my very first lesson in love. *Lost love.* I begin to believe that love means loss.

I finally finish school sometime during the middle of the Easter term, after my final retake. I follow my parents back to Barbados and straight into a war zone.

Mum is as volatile as a feral, caged animal and Dad is even more nervous and indecisive. He has just been made redundant from his job as a hotel time-share manager, a job that has lasted less than a year. He's decided instead to work with an artist friend of his selling hand-painted maps of the Caribbean islands. This means a huge drop in his salary and he asks Mum to dismiss our two gardeners, our cook and our lovely housekeeper. My mother is absolutely furious. She can't bear the thought of losing all her staff. Not because she and Dad will have to do all the housework and look after the garden themselves, but mostly because of how it will appear to her friends.

While I've been away, my parents have acquired two Weimaraner dogs, one male and one female. My mother has been trying to breed them, unsuccessfully. There is only one surviving puppy from three consecutive litters. His name is Xavier. Xavier keeps me sane in those days, post-school. His breath is sweet and he is soft and warm in my lap.

Every day, my mother throws my father's clothes out of the front door and onto the flagstone path.

'Get out! Get out, *you useless shit!*' I hear her screaming at him. 'Pack your bags and *leave!*' she shrieks, daily. 'Go and find a *proper* job!'

One day, without saying a word my father picks up all of his clothes, which are strewn across the front path, and brings them back inside. This isn't at all unusual. I have seen him do this several times. What happens next, on the other hand, *is*.

When he finally emerges from my parents' bedroom, he's carrying a suitcase and a large carrier bag. He turns back briefly and his eyes meet mine, for just a fleeting moment, before he walks out of the front door for the very last time.

'*Don't leave me, Dad!*' I want to scream. But instead, I say absolutely nothing. It's a lesson I have learned from him. Keep quiet, because it only makes matters worse.

The atmosphere in the house after my father leaves soon becomes unbearable. With him gone, there is no one to talk to. My sister and brothers are still away at boarding school and my mother and I very rarely converse. My only interaction with her is to do as I am told, mostly with my mouth shut.

'See what kind of a man your father is, Rachel?' she snaps at me as we sit down for supper one evening. 'The useless kind who leaves you when the going gets tough.'

I want to jump up from the table and throw my plate at her face. But I say nothing. I don't even look up at her. She has no idea whatsoever that my father has left because she made it absolutely impossible for him to stay. She is the sole reason that the going got tough.

The very next day, I call my father in desperation and plead with him to pick me up.

'Dad, please come and get me. I can't stay here. I'll go crazy. *Please!*'

I am relieved when he does. However, my mother refuses to let me leave without taking all three dogs with me. Therefore, later that afternoon, with our two Weimaraners in the back of my father's car and little Xavier sitting in my lap in the front, my father glances over at me and starts the engine. Only the dogs seem to be excited. I am terrified that my mother will come out of the house and try and stop me from leaving. To my great relief, she remains indoors. My heart is hammering away inside my chest as we drive out through the gates for the very last time. I vow that I will never, *ever*, live under the same roof as her again.

A motley crew, we are: me, my father and our three dogs. As for our new living arrangements, my father has begged a favour from a friend with an empty upstairs flat on a quiet residential street. She agrees that he can move in temporarily. Somehow, I don't think she would have agreed quite so readily had she known that we would all be living together in her very small upstairs apartment. My father, all three dogs and me (although Xavier is very small.) However, my father knew I couldn't stay for one more day with my mother. She was completely unhinged, spewing venom like an extra in *The Exorcist.* She hated *everyone*… most of all, my father.

Now, my father is a terrible cook. The kitchen has always been my mother's department and cooking is the one thing she does really well, if you discount some of her more adventurous concoctions, like stuffed hearts and cou-cou.

Dear God! I can only describe cou-cou as something akin to snotty mashed potato with much less flavour (my sincere apologies to all my West Indian, cou-cou-eating friends). It is truly *revolting!* And boy did I revolt when she once served it to me…

I am four or five years old. My mother is standing over me, forcing me to eat and I'm struggling to swallow the small forkful I've just put in my mouth. I've managed to eat almost half of the cou-cou on my plate, but I can feel my mouth filling up with saliva as a wave of nausea washes over me. I desperately want to spit it back out. I look up at my mother with wide, pleading eyes.

'Don't you even think about it, Rachel!' she threatens, her finger jabbing very close to my face. 'Swallow it, now!' she yells. I am terrified of her but even more frightened that I'm going to be sick. And right then, I am sick, straight back onto my plate. Snotty vomit it is, now. Mum looks horrified. That pleases me no end.

And that is the last time she forces me to eat anything. A small victory for a small me...

I will never forget our first supper together in that upstairs flat. Dad has bought some stewing steak, carrots and potatoes to make a hearty stew. The meat is like shoe leather, although the carrots and the potatoes are just about edible. None of that matters. The laughter, joy and freedom we both experience together on my first night away from Mum? Well, you just can't put a price on that.

CHAPTER 6

The next day, I wake up in a panic, remembering that I've left a brand new portable stereo behind, one I've bought for my brother's birthday. It is huge, with two detachable speakers on either side; a Ghetto Blaster which cost all my savings. I don't want to risk leaving it, not with my mother's penchant for stereo smashing. It's only a question of *when*, rather than *if*, she will break it in a temper.

I borrow Dad's car and I drive back home, hoping and praying Mum will be out and I can sneak in and out, undetected. My heart sinks when I see her car in the drive. *Damn!*

I knock, although I have my own keys. I'm thinking I'd better avoid doing anything to set her off and marching in, unannounced, is a definite no-no.

She comes to the door, looking haggard and drawn.

'What the hell do you want?' she says, in a low, gravelly voice.

I clear my throat. 'I bought Casper a present. A stereo. I-I forgot to bring it with me yesterday.' Casper is in the very fortunate position of being over four thousand miles away at boarding school. 'I'm here to collect it. I'll be very quick,' I say hopefully, but my mother refuses outright.

'I'll give it to him when he's back,' she snaps, slamming the door in my face.

My heart begins to beat very fast and I can feel the familiar shot of adrenaline coursing through my veins.

I am *not* going to leave without the stereo.

I put my key in the door and I open it, just in time to find my mother attempting to remove the stereo from my bedroom. I run over to her, grab the handle and with all of my strength, I manage to pull it out of my mother's grasp. I hold it away from her with one arm and with the other, I attempt to keep her, quite literally, at arm's length as I retreat backwards towards the door.

'I am taking this with me, Mum,' I say with steely determination, as she claws away at me like a wild animal. Like someone possessed. And then she launches herself at me.

'You little bitch!' she screams, her face contorted with rage. I am ashamed to say that my mother and I are now having a full-scale brawl on the utility room floor. I'm doing my level best to fend her off while she's doing all she can to hurt me.

Eventually, I twist away as she sinks her teeth into my upper arm and bites down hard. It gives me the edge and enough time to get to my feet, with her still biting down on my arm, now drawing blood. *My mother.* She lets go, and in a split second, with every ounce of my strength I push her away from me, and I run from the house with the stereo still intact. I jump into Dad's car, start the engine, and I get the hell out of there as quickly as I can.

I don't remember driving back to the flat. My heart is pumping so fast, I can hear it pounding in my ears. I don't think I've ever felt anything quite like it in all of my life. The utter fury and hatred I felt for her in that moment was overwhelming. However, I'm glad that I stood up to her. I'm glad I fought back.

When I show the injury to Dad, he looks up at me and almost bursts into tears. I go and look in the mirror to see it properly. I have to hold my arm up and slightly across my body, as she's bitten the soft underside of my upper arm. There are bright red teeth marks in a semi-circle and, all around the injury, a dark bruise is beginning to show. It looks angry. Like her.

She is deeply disturbed, my mother. I know this already but what I haven't realised, until that day, is just *how* disturbed. Neither my father nor I say anything about it again.

Later that evening, as I'm standing in the shower, attempting to wash away her venom, I suddenly realise what it is that triggers my mother's behaviour. If ever she feels she is losing control, she goes berserk. And in the previous twenty-four hours, I think it finally dawned on my mother that she has nothing whatsoever left to control. *Not one thing*.

Dad and I move a few times after that, accepting the charity of several well-meaning friends, and I see Mum only once during that time, when she turns up unexpectedly in yet another one of her rages.

We are living on the far side of the island in a friend's two-bedroomed annexe. I'm not sure exactly how she has found us, but she has. She doesn't knock. She just marches in, uninvited. Her insanity peaks.

'You left me in the *shit!*' she screams at my father. And then she takes her pants down, squats on the floor and urinates right then and there in front of us. Dad says nothing at all. He just leaves the room and goes outside to get a mop and bucket. Mum has already left by the time he returns. Oddly, I am feeling very little. Relief, I suppose, that she's gone.

Life is much calmer after that.

Dad and I finally settle into an upstairs flat of our own. I choose some cheerful tropical fabric to recover a tired old sofa and chairs and we turn the space into a happy, cosy home. There are three bedrooms, a small living room and an enormous kitchen. Downstairs, at the back of the building, there is only a very small yard where the dogs can run around. It's a far cry from the three acres or the long walks on the golf course they've been used to, but we are taking care of them as best we can.

Until one day, Dad comes back from work and he wants to speak to me. I feel a flash of fear. I can see something is wrong.

'Rach, we need to rehome the dogs. It's not fair having all three of them living here. There just isn't the space. They deserve better.' He looks at me. *Hangdog.* I would probably laugh if my heart wasn't on the floor. Of course, I know he's right.

I go and find the three of them, knowing that we haven't got long left together. I want to pat them all, to smooth their coats and rub behind their ears. All three are lying in the yard in the late afternoon sun. Xavier is curled into his mum. He is dreaming. I watch his tiny paws twitching. The thick post of the washing line casts a long, thin shadow across their bodies, dividing them in two. They sleep peacefully. My heart constricts.

It isn't long before a friend of both my parents agrees to take them on. She wants to take the dogs back to her main home in Switzerland at the end of the month. My father tells me she is a countess and she lives in an enormous mansion on the banks of Lake Leman. She also has a Boxer, so they will have a new playmate. I feel happy about that.

Much too soon, it's time to say goodbye. All three are standing in the back of the car. Lolling tongues, tails wagging like whips. They think they're off for a walk on the beach. They lick my hand, over and over, as I stroke each of their heads. They have no idea that this is the last time they will see me. For some reason, this makes it so much harder. I am heartbroken. Tears well up and stream down my face. My vision is blurred. Dad squeezes my arm gently and he closes the car door. I have a pain in my chest, as if I've been stabbed. This is utter *shit*. The very last thing I see is Xavier's wet nose pressed up against the rear windscreen as Dad's car disappears out of sight. Somehow, this all seems familiar. Déjà vu.

Several weeks later, I have mixed feelings when we finally receive a photo of them all, settled and clearly happy, posing for the camera on the sweeping front steps of the countess's huge house, with their new Boxer friend. They look well fed and happy, but I miss them all terribly, especially Xavier. I touch the photo. He's almost fully grown in the photograph. I hardly recognise him.

As for me, I find a new job working for a local company selling advertising space for a directory in both Barbados and Grenada. *I love it*, and it suits me perfectly. I'm able to work from home and I still have a lot of free time to go to the beach and meet up with my friends, which I do every afternoon. The job is a total breeze.

My boss and I fly to Grenada for two weeks each year and he books us into a beautiful hotel set in lush, tropical gardens arranged in tiers, with flashes of brightly coloured hibiscus spilling over the smooth, whitewashed walls. The view is spectacular. The hotel has a terracotta tiled roof and a 180-degree view of the sea. The food is especially good. Immediately, I fall in love with the island and the people. They all seem so happy. Wide toothy grins, some with a flash of gold. They make me feel welcome. Suddenly, I am all grown up. In reality I'm only just twenty.

I have new zest for life. I work in the morning and then I drive down to the beach in the late afternoon for a swim. Often, I stay and watch the sun set. Sometimes alone, sometimes with friends. I am free to come and go as I please.

Dad and I are having lunch together at the Coach House one day, when I finally pluck up the courage to ask him straight.

I look up from my pepperpot stew. 'Why did you never stand up to Mum?'

He stops his fork, mid-air, before it reaches his mouth. He puts it back down on his plate. Clattering. A lost mouthful, tumbling off the four silver prongs. He picks up his beer. A bead of condensation drips silently onto the table as he drinks, his throat moving in and out with each gulp. He places the glass back down, holding the rim between fingers and thumb, swivelling it around, left to right and then slowly, right to left, before answering.

'Rach, when I was married the first time around to Pat, before I met your mother in Jamaica, we often had physical fights. I *hated* it. She would fly off the handle at the slightest thing and lay into me, fists first. Back then, I would fight back, defend myself...' He pauses to take another large swig of his beer. 'When your mother and I met, we began to have disagreements very early on. She was quick to lose her temper, the same as Pat, and if I ever retaliated, she became much, *much* worse, lashing out at me like some crazy, wild thing. I vowed then that I would *never* fight back, because I was in love with her. Rach, I needed to find a way to diffuse the situation. *Quickly.* I swore I would never be violent again. *Ever.* I've kept that promise from that day to this. I was terrified she might do something terrible when she got that angry. Still am. Not my concern anymore, though. *Thank God.*'

I look up at him. Suddenly old. He is broken. His eyes are filled with tears. But my heart has hardened to stone. I get up from the table, my chair scraping noisily on the terracotta tiled floor, the only noise as I make to leave without saying one more word.

I never see Mum although sometimes, when I'm in the supermarket, I begin to feel paranoid. The hairs on the back of my neck stand up and I swing around, fully expecting to see her angry face pushing a trolley full of bleach and polish. I often worry I'm going to bump into her in one of the aisles or in the checkout queue. But so far, I haven't.

I live this life for four years, encased in a bubble of bliss, and then one morning I wake up and something feels different. I am lying on my side in bed, listening to the birds outside my window, with the sheet pulled over my shoulders. I look at the clock on my bedside table. It's 7:49 am. I think about work and I wrinkle up my nose. I turn onto my back and fling one arm out from under the sheet, with my palm flat against the mattress. I begin to pat it, absent-mindedly. I really can't be bothered today. I am restless.

I am experiencing what the locals refer to as "rock fever" – when island life begins to drive you a little crazy. Some call it boredom, and yes, I realise that I'm bored. I'm also fed up with the heat. I think of England and of all my school friends. I haven't thought about them for a while and I've been terrible at keeping in touch. I miss them.

Later that day, I make a long-distance call.

CHAPTER 7

I pick up my heavy tan suitcase from the carousel using both hands and haul it onto a metal trolley. Its 6:30 in the morning and I'm in the baggage hall at Gatwick Airport. Robyn, my good friend from school, is probably already here. I'll be staying with her and her boyfriend Gus, for three weeks. Penny is away in Portugal.

'Oh, my gosh, Rach! You're so brown!' Robyn squeals as I walk out into the arrival hall. She throws her arms around me and gives me a squeeze. She smells of Chanel No 5 and cheap deodorant. I haven't slept much on the flight and my eyes are scratchy. So am I. 'How was the flight?' she asks, with a smile.

'Pretty shit. I didn't sleep a wink,' I say, stifling a yawn. It's July and already I'm feeling the drop in temperature. I stop the trolley, unzip my suitcase and remove a grey fleece hoodie. I pull it over my head. My hair is all over the place but I don't care.

'You cold?' Robyn looks surprised.

'Yep,' is all I say.

Eventually, we find her white Fiat Panda in the vast car park and Robyn helps me lift my case into the boot. It fits. Just. Robyn is now on her third takeaway coffee and she's talking non-stop. Mostly, I grunt in response. Her voice is beginning to irritate me. Finally, we slip into silence and the next thing I am aware of is Robyn shaking my arm.

'We're here, sleepyhead,' she says, leaning in towards me. *I must have dozed off.* I stretch – an almost impossible task in the front of her car, but at least I'm feeling a little better. Robyn leads me into her boyfriend's terraced house. She shows me into the second bedroom. It's Gus's weights room and there is a mattress on the floor for me. It smells of antiseptic.

'Rach, I need to go to work now, but make yourself at home. I'll be back around four. Gus may be back before me. There's tea and coffee, et cetera, in the kitchen.' And with that, she leaves.

It's quiet. Deathly quiet. I'm feeling out of sorts. Gus's house is dark and all the curtains are drawn. I'm used to bright sunlight. I'm now wondering if this trip was a good idea.

Exactly one week later, I'm sitting in the back of Robyn's car as she skilfully manoeuvres into a parking space, crunching the gravel under her tyres outside a local country pub. Gus is sitting in the passenger seat directly in front of me. He has an odd-shaped head, like a tall box, and his hair is flat. I don't like his aftershave – it reminds me of a pot pourri refill. We're here because one of Gus's friends, Pierce, is playing in a band tonight. We met when he dropped in to see Gus a few days ago. I thought he was cute. He smells of washing powder. Persil, I think.

Robyn lets me out of the back of the car and as we head over to the entrance, our footsteps crunch noisily on the gravel. Robyn and Gus are discussing holidays. I'm quiet. It's already packed inside and very smoky as we make our way through the crowd and over to the bar. Gus orders drinks for the three of us. He flirts with the barmaid. When he smiles, you can see the crow's feet in the corner of his eyes. Robyn isn't impressed. She doesn't smile at all. Gus hands me and Robyn a glass of wine each; she has white, I have red. Gus has ordered a Guinness, which spills over onto the bar, thick cream on varnished wood.

The band is about to start and the three of us make our way down the side of the room towards the front, to watch. A few odd notes belt out from the massive speakers on either side of the band, which makes me jump. It's *loud*. The sound vibrates right through me. I can feel it in my teeth. There is a whoop from the crowd and someone in front of me spills her drink. It splashes on my foot. She apologises, but I'm not concerned, because I've just spotted Pierce. He's on drums. I can see the veins standing out on his forearms as he smashes the hell out of them. The band is fantastic. I'm surprised. Pierce's eyes are closed and his head tilts up towards the spotlights. At that moment, I begin to feel the stirrings of something almost forgotten, something I haven't felt since Frank. I like the feeling but almost immediately, I am scared by it.

When the band finishes the set, Pierce bounds over to us and greets Gus by slapping him on the shoulder. He plants a sweaty kiss on Robyn's cheek and does the same to me.

'Buy you a drink?' I ask, leaning in over the noise of the packed pub.

'Cheers, that'd be great,' he replies with a huge grin. 'It's hot as hell up there.' He thumbs in the direction of his drums, wiping the sweat from his forehead. *It's hot as hell right here,* I'm thinking to myself. I feel a little flustered but before I say anything stupid, I ask Robyn and Gus what they'd like to drink before picking my way through to the bar.

By the end of the night, Pierce has invited me over to his house for a nightcap and I accept without hesitation. I've probably had too much to drink already, but I really don't care. I'm flying high. The wine and my attraction to Pierce are an intoxicating mix. I climb into Pierce's silver TVR and we speed off into the night. *Yee-ha!*

I am on my third glass of wine, with my leg draped over Pierce's as we recline, half-sitting, half-lying, on his sofa. Nina Simone is playing softly in the background. The room is silently spinning and Pierce leans towards me and presses his lips onto mine. My heart leaps and I respond by kissing him back, gently at first. Pierce pulls me down flat and eases his weight on top of me, kissing me harder on the mouth, his desire now obvious. I want him badly. I don't care that I've only known him for a few days.

We pull each other's clothes off quickly, clumsily almost, and Pierce positions himself on top of me, only this time there is nothing between us except the heat of our skin pressing together. I am really quite drunk and everything feels like a dream. I'm not sure what's real anymore.

The dawn has begun to lighten the day behind Pierce's sitting room blinds. I become aware of this through my congealed mascara. I am naked, squeezed between him and the back of his sofa. My head is pounding and I feel sick.

'Dear God, Rach,' I think to myself, shamefully, as I attempt to climb over a still-sleeping Pierce. I make it to his bathroom and lock the door. I look at myself in the mirror and am horrified at the person looking back at me. My makeup is badly smudged, staining my eyes black and purple, like a heavy rock guitarist. My skin is otherwise a greyish white and my lips are almost blue. Suddenly, the room spins and I feel a wave of nausea washing over me. I run to the loo, which,

thankfully, is already open. *Praise be.* I throw up loudly three times and then I sit down heavily. My skin makes an odd thwack on the cold tiles. I wipe the tears from my eyes. My fingers are black. I want to be anywhere other than sitting naked on Pierce's bathroom floor, feeling wretched.

'Pull yourself together, girl,' I tell myself sternly, as I rise very carefully onto unsteady feet. I decide to take a shower and wash my hair, which proves to be an excellent decision, because I feel considerably better by the time I've stepped out and wrapped a towel around me. I wipe the steam off the mirror and this time I look halfway to normal. I breathe a sigh of relief. And then I heave. I desperately need a glass of water.

Pierce is still asleep by the time I manage to find all my clothes. I'm relieved I'm able to dress without him watching me. In the cold light of day, the alcohol-fuelled confidence I felt the night before has completely disappeared, and I am now seriously regretting the decision I made to come back for a nightcap.

I am in the kitchen, looking around for two mugs, when Pierce appears, naked and gorgeous, in the kitchen doorway. He looks fresh and bright, with no outward signs of a hangover, unlike me. We chat for a while over coffee, which he makes in the end, and then he suggests dropping me home, as he is due at his parents' for Sunday lunch. A very small part of me wants him to invite me along, but I am still feeling terrible and, really, all I want is to get back to Robyn and Gus's spare room and climb onto my bed (mattress) for the rest of the day. Which I do.

When my three weeks are up, I make the rather foolish, romantic decision not to return to Barbados because I want to spend more time with Pierce. Now that I've had time to acclimatise, I realise just how much I've missed living in England.

I call my boss in Barbados and set up an interview for a friend of mine who I know is looking for work. She can do my job standing on her head, and within a week, she's taken over from me. My bridges are now well and truly burned and I am left with the very real issue of having no money, no job and no fixed abode.

It doesn't take long for Robyn to go off the idea of me crashing on Gus's spare room floor. It's been almost three months and she now wants me to leave. I can't really blame her. I haven't been able to find a job as yet, and I'm beginning to doubt my rather hasty decision to stay in England. This is a very low point in my life. The weather is bloody miserable, I have no winter clothes, and very soon I will be homeless. I ask the Universe for help.

The next morning, I wake up and Robyn is standing in the doorway.

'I can't get to work,' she says flatly. 'There's been a bloody hurricane and all the trees are down in every direction.'

I've slept soundly all night. Better, in fact, than I've slept in weeks. Strangely, the rather exceptional weather has breathed new life into me. I can't really explain it, but I see the storm as a sign, and I feel motivated for the first time in weeks to make something of my life in England.

That afternoon, I call one of Pierce's friends, Tammy, someone I met at one of his gigs. We'd really hit it off, and I'd been talking to her about my less-than-ideal sleeping arrangements. She tells me she is housesitting for her employer, and if I ever need an escape, I can always stay and keep her company.

'Yes, of course the offer still stands, Rach. It'll be great to have the company,' Tammy says cheerfully. 'Last time I checked, they were clearing trees off the A224. Get packed and hopefully, I'll be with you soon.'

I sigh with relief as I put the phone back in its cradle and go and pack my suitcase.

Robyn is in the sitting room with Gus as I stand in the doorway, hovering with my bags. I'm feeling more than a little uncomfortable. I clear my throat.

'Tammy has offered to put me up for a bit and I-I really want to thank you for allowing me to stay with you both for so long. I really do appreciate it.'

They stand up and give me a hug. Gus seems genuinely surprised and a little upset to learn that I am leaving, but Robyn looks relieved.

I find myself sofa surfing for some time before landing a telesales job for a local newspaper. It pays well enough and very soon I'm able to take up lodgings in a cosy home on a quiet street of mostly semi-detached houses. The owner is hardly ever at home. Mostly, he stays with his girlfriend in London during the week, which means I often have the house to myself. This suits me perfectly, because when he's at home, I don't sleep very well. He makes love to his pretty, although slightly cross-eyed, girlfriend, who screams as if she is being murdered when she climaxes. She's so loud I wake up in a panic. I feel invaded. As if I've got nits. Thankfully, they don't take long.

Pierce comes to stay with me most nights of the week, after we've been out to the pub together. For a time, I am happy. And then I miss my period.

This is highly unusual as I'm regular as clockwork. Twenty-eight days precisely. Today is day thirty-three and still, my period hasn't arrived. The next day, I walk into town to the local chemist and I buy myself a pregnancy kit. I don't look at the grey-haired woman on the till because I'm embarrassed about my purchase. I avoid looking at her because I think she may have a "you're-a-bit-young-to-be-pregnant" expression on her face. I slink off home and go straight upstairs to the bathroom, with my heart in my mouth.

I read the instructions carefully and open the foil wrapper, pulling out the white plastic test stick. I undo the cap and pee on one end of the stick, as instructed. Replacing the cap carefully, I move to sit on the edge of the bath and hold the test stick up, so I can see the small window. My heart begins to beat rapidly as a solid blue line slowly appears. *So far so good,* I think naïvely, until another, much fainter second blue line appears, making a cross with the first blue line.

Shit! I can't believe it. I'm not even twenty-one yet and I've only just found a job and begun to feel settled again. I call Penny straightaway.

'Penny, I'm pregnant,' I wail over the phone.

'Bloody hell, Rach! What are you going to do?' she replies. We speak for over an hour, with me mostly in tears, but by the end of our conversation, Penny has convinced me to have a termination.

Before we say goodbye, I make Penny promise me she won't tell anyone, especially not Robyn, who I think will likely tell Gus, and then Pierce might ultimately find out. I decide that this *must never happen*. I've grown very fond of Pierce, to the point I feel that certain I'm in love with him. I'm very worried he may see me in a different light, despite his obvious involvement. I know for certain that Pierce isn't ready to be a father.

Strangely, and more than a little coincidentally, Pierce begins to cool towards me almost immediately after that. He makes excuses about coming over or says he can't meet me up at the pub. I feel sure he must have heard about my condition. *Our* condition. But I get the message, loud and clear: he's no longer interested, whether he knows or not. It dawns on me I must have meant nothing to him and, although my heart is breaking, a few weeks later, I go ahead with the termination because I'm just not ready to be a mother. Certainly not a single mother.

Life never really feels the same again for me after that, not for a very long time. I go through the motions: work, home, eat, sleep, and somewhere, deep within me, I know that more than the promise of new life has been lost. A part of me seems lost forever. A royal princess is born on exactly the same day that my unborn baby would have been due — the eighth day of the eighth month in nineteen eighty-eight. An almost cruelly memorable date.

As for Pierce, I can't really blame him for anything other than being as irresponsible as me about using (*not* using!) birth control. I'm almost relieved when I hear he's moved away.

CHAPTER 8

I focus on work and move through the ranks quickly — as swiftly as I move homes, it seems — until I finally settle into a shared house in a beautiful village in the countryside, with two other professional women. When I have a day off, I go and sit on the village green under one of the large chestnut trees opposite the house and I watch the children from the primary school next door playing in the sunshine. They laugh with such unencumbered joy. This image stays with me, but I'm unsure why.

A few weeks after I move in, I'm introduced to Ben in the local pub. Almost immediately, I can tell he likes me, but I'm wary about getting involved with anyone after Pierce.

Ben is cheeky, charming and very, *very* persistent. I love his sense of humour and we spend the majority of our time laughing together. In no time at all, we've become the best of friends.

It takes less than a year before Ben and I are officially an item, and two more for me to decide I want to marry him. Although, if I'm being brutally honest, I don't fancy him. That issue doesn't really concern me, however, because I truly believe that Ben is perfect husband material and I get on very well with his mum. He is my soulmate and that's more than good enough for me.

I often talk to Ben about getting married, but each time I mention it, he becomes restless and changes the subject. *Quickly.* By now, we've been together for almost four years and I'm ready to make a commitment. The truth is, I'd like to have a baby.

Towards the end of our fourth year together, I receive a very strange call from Penny late one Saturday morning. She and a friend of hers from work have been out clubbing in London for the first time. Penny tells me she hasn't been to bed yet and it's now eleven in the morning. She sounds completely wired. She laughs, saying she was offered a pill in the club, which made her want to dance all night long. The drug she's taken is called Ecstasy and it's made her and her friend Tiffany, feel *bloody amazing*. She urges me to come along with them the following weekend and try one.

I must admit, I am tempted.

Penny and Tiffany are clearly having a fantastic time and after a few weeks of sitting on the fence, I finally give in, get my glad rags on and go out with them.

That night is an eye-opener. It's a night I will *never* forget.

It brings to an end the final chapter of my young, relatively innocent life and heralds the dawn of an entirely new era of garage music, drugs, all-night dancing and male strippers. Without a backward glance, I leave Ben and any thoughts of marriage or children behind me.

Penny and I take it in turns to drive. Tonight, it's my turn. First, we drop Tiffany's daughter off at her father's in Croydon. Then, we head up to London in my Renault 5, dolled up to the nines, our makeup impeccable. *Glamorous.* The latest garage music is blaring from my speakers. Penny is sitting next to me in the front passenger seat. She is singing at the top of her lungs. In my rear-view mirror, Tiffany is dancing so hard on the back seat that she's making the entire car rock. We stop at a set of traffic lights and I look over at the car next to me. There's a young man sitting at the wheel with his eyes on stalks. I laugh and blow him a kiss before speeding off.

It takes us almost an hour to reach the club. We find a suitable parking place and the three of us are immediately waved past a long queue of people by one of the doormen who fancies Tiffany. She is flirting outrageously as we strut past him into the club.

I feel like a celebrity, every single week.

We remove our coats in the cloakroom. Tonight, I'm wearing a Jean Paul Gaultier-style silver basque with black velvet hot pants. I'm well over six foot in my high-heeled suede boots. My hair is a mane of bouncing chestnut curls, freshly washed and shiny under the club lights. I flick it over to one side and behind my right shoulder. Tiffany is wearing a fishnet catsuit with nothing but a black bra and chainmail thong. She has a fantastic figure, shapely with a tiny waist. Her bleached-blonde bob fans out, perfectly straight as she looks from left to right, checking out who's already here. Penny is rocking the Sixties look. She's poured herself into a tight-fitting pair of leggings with ruffled bottoms and finished it off with a tie top with ruffled sleeves. Both are made out of the same psychedelic print, which makes my head spin if I look at it for too long. She looks like a young Britt Eckland. Prettier, in fact. We are dressed like this for attention. We thrive on it.

I follow Penny over to the bar for a bottle of water. We never drink alcohol. Very occasionally, we have a jelly shot, but I'm not very keen on them. Then, the three of us make our way to the bathroom at the back of the club and enter the same cubicle together. Penny pulls a small tinfoil package out of her bra and unwraps three white pills. She hands one to Tiffany, one to me, and the other she holds in her teeth as she waits for a swig from the water bottle.

We flush the toilet and the three of us leave the bathroom. Job done.

We strut through the bar and onto the dance floor on the opposite side of the club. It's dark in here and it takes a moment for my eyes to adjust. It's impossible to see the colour of the walls. Everything looks black, with the occasional pulsation of light. The music is pumping. It's already packed.

We find a space at the front of the dance floor and we wait to 'come up'. It takes about twenty minutes. The feeling creeps up from the centre of my head and washes over my entire body, like goosebumps in slow motion. My mind begins to expand. It swallows up the light and the darkness of the dance floor and reaches out in every direction, encompassing the entire club, extending ever-outward. I feel it all. London. England. Earth. Like a satellite in space. I am expanding at the speed of light. As I dance, the feeling of euphoria and love I have for everyone is overwhelming. I'm flying with both feet planted firmly on the dance floor. Penny shouts over the music.

'How's your E?'

'I'm off my tits!' I reply. I can't stop dancing. I am the Universe.

'I'm totally fucked,' Tiffany says. Her pupils are huge. She laughs.

We become part of the music. Time rolls away. It no longer has meaning. It is only possible to *be* in the present moment as the entire room of dancers becomes one mass of pulsating rhythm, moving in time to the beat as music blares from the huge speakers on either side of the room. We dance. Sweat drips from our bodies. The DJ takes us higher and higher as he mixes dance tracks together, seamlessly blending one into the next. He is Master of the Crowd. The Pied Piper. We revere him. We are rats.

This happens every single weekend for almost a year. I'm nearly twenty-six and no longer feel despondent over my stagnating relationship with Ben. In fact, I want to be single again. As for wanting a baby, well, that idea just seems ridiculous. I want to be free.

While I'm having the time of my life in London, Ben's attention is diverted by a pretty young barmaid in our local pub. He whisks her off to Spain almost immediately after we agree to a separation. My initial sadness is quickly forgotten with the ecstasy, quite literally, of the club. Another love lost. Only this time, I've found something better. Something that makes me feel love.

CHAPTER 9

It's during one of our regular Friday night jaunts to the club that I meet José. He is gorgeous, muscular, and we both have exactly the same long, dark, curly hair. We laugh when we see each other, like old friends meeting up after a long absence. He is part of a London male strip troupe, and the entire troupe are with him in the club, dancing bare-chested in the bar area.

José has an incredible physique. He's tanned, toned, lean, and *oh, my goodness,* can he dance! We spend the whole night together, dancing, until they turn the lights on and the music off at ten the next morning.

Even then, we carry on dancing, our pupils huge. We make our own beat, clapping to a silent track, which only we can hear inside our heads. Despite the bright lights, I am entirely uninhibited. There is no judgment here. We're all connected. We're not ready to be unplugged. Not yet.

Eventually, the crowd breaks up and we slowly disperse, herded out by yawning bouncers. Before we leave, José and I exchange phone numbers. Penny, Tiffany and I drive home, even more excited than we were on our way up to the club. It's been a truly fantastic evening. One of the best.

A few days later, José and I speak on the phone. I'm wondering if he really is as attractive as I remember in my drug-altered state. I've thought about little else since. We chat for a few minutes and José invites me to join him one evening at work. He promises to take me out for dinner afterwards. It sounds like fun and so, later that week, I jump on a train and I meet him up in London at a private club in the West End.

I am relieved to find him exactly as I remember, with a huge cheeky grin and an exquisite physique clearly visible through his tight-fitting t-shirt. I feel a little light-headed.

He leads me through a crowd of several women who are already undressing him with their eyes and over to the bar, where he orders me a drink. Then he finds me a seat in a quiet corner of the room. He kisses me on the cheek and says he'll return to me after the show. I feel very conspicuous in that room; I'm sitting on my own, nervously sipping my drink as I watch the rising excitement from the gaggle of women surrounding me. They're clearly on a hen night and it's obvious several of them are already drunk. The anticipation in the room is palpable.

Twenty minutes later, José appears to the sound of a well-known strip-appropriate song. He's holding a microphone, clearly at ease, grinning from ear to ear.

'Hello, *la-dies!*' he shouts to the crowd. They all jump to their feet and begin to scream. I immediately feel a strong urge to slink off into the dark night. This is a completely new experience for me, witnessing women behaving like lusty animals. It is really quite unnerving.

After a while, however, I stand up so I can see more. José is working the crowd like a true professional. Item by item, he removes his clothing, until all he's wearing is a miniscule canary-yellow thong. His body is incredible. There is not one ounce of fat on him and he has bulging, glistening muscles. *Wow, impressive.* I giggle to myself. The mojito is taking effect.

So is José's body. I begin to move with the music while my nearly naked date asks a room full of crazed women if they want him to remove the last piece of his clothing. *Of course.*

'*Ye-e-es!* Off, off, *off*!' they all scream.

Dear God. He's not taking everything off? Surely?

The women are frightening. They look at José with raw, unadulterated lust in their eyes. Slowly, very slowly, he removes his thong to reveal himself, semi-erect. He thrusts provocatively at them and they go wild. I sit down, hard.

Shit. He's completely naked, and clearly aroused by all the attention. Suddenly, I'm afraid. *What the hell have I got myself into here?*

José finishes his performance and retreats through a door at the back of the room. I down my drink and seriously toy with the idea of leaving. My heart is pounding inside my chest, *not* from excitement. I'm now wondering what José might be expecting from me on our date. It seems clear that he's utterly uninhibited. The kind of explicit flaunting that I've just witnessed from him is entirely alien to me. *Is he expecting to have sex with me tonight?* Before I have time to freak myself out any more, there he is, standing over me. He's obviously showered, as his long hair is damp and he smells fresh and clean. He's grinning at me and then he leans back and laughs, heartily – a big belly laugh.

'Don't look so frightened, Rach,' he pats my shoulder reassuringly. 'They like to let their hair down, don't they?' He laughs again, looking around at the women who have, mostly, returned to their tables. Some are now at the bar and a few others are on the dance floor. They are completely ignoring him. He might as well be invisible.

'Shall we head out?' He thumbs towards the exit and cocks his head to one side.

'Yes, please,' I blurt out, immediately jumping to my feet. I feel relieved he hasn't realised that my fear is rooted in what he might be expecting of me during the remainder of our date. I'm also wondering where he's going to take me next, and how I might be able to cut the night short and retreat home on the train.

It's an enormous relief, therefore, when José suggests we walk the short distance into Chinatown for supper. He guides me to a Chinese restaurant he knows well and he explains that the food is simple but delicious. He's right. The atmosphere in the restaurant is lively and the smell of cooking makes my mouth water. I'm suddenly aware of how hungry I am.

The evening proves to be very enjoyable. We talk about everything, from our experiences of growing up overseas, to work and religion. José is the perfect host and he's extremely funny. We laugh *a lot* that evening, and when it comes time for me to leave, he escorts me swiftly through the streets of London to the train station, a brisk twenty-minute stroll away. When we arrive, I only have a few moments to board the last train home and José wastes no time in giving me a huge bear hug and a swift peck on the cheek.

'I had a *great* night tonight, Rach,' he says, beaming from ear to ear. 'Let's do it again soon.' With that, he claps his hands together, gives me a small bow and turns on his heel to walk the short distance back to a queue of night owls, waiting for black cabs outside the front of the station.

I only just make it through the doors of the train before I hear the loud release of the brakes. I stumble through the carriage as it's pulling out of the station and I soon find an empty seat.

I settle down for the journey home with my mind in overdrive, replaying the evening over and over again. What a night! My jaw is physically aching from so much laughing. Even *that* thought makes me laugh again. I'm also relieved that my earlier fears about José's intentions are completely unfounded. Despite everything I witnessed earlier, he behaved like the perfect gentleman.

José and I spend a lot of time together over the next few months. On several occasions, I end up back at his place, in his bed. But we never make love. Not in those early months, at least. Initially, I think he finds my reluctance to sleep with him amusing, but after a while I can see he respects my decision and he never presses me. We slip into an easy platonic friendship and this suits me perfectly. The truth is, I am completely and utterly besotted with José. I'm not sure if it's love or lust, but I think it's probably a combination of the two. However, I'm absolutely determined not to become another notch on his bedpost. There are already too many notches for my liking. I don't ever want to lose José and by staying in the friend zone, I truly believe I'm protecting myself from getting hurt.

I go along to some of his strip nights and I sit in the audience. Sometimes I go with Penny, Tiffany and Robyn and we watch him and the rest of the troupe in action. The women in the audience go wild, screaming, and behaving in a way I still find shocking. It's not uncommon to find the odd one or two making their way backstage after a show, offering to have sex with a member of the troupe. José laughs it off, but I can see he feels uncomfortable whenever I am there to witness one of the troupe disappearing into a back room with an unknown female from the audience.

We leave together after he's showered and changed. Today, we are back in the safety of his car and I pluck up the courage to ask him if he's ever had sex with any of the brazen women backstage. He doesn't answer my question directly, but I'm left in no doubt when he laughs and shrugs. It's this observation in particular that stops me from having sex with José, because I am now seriously concerned that he might have some kind of STD.

Penny, Tiffany and I continue to frequent the nightclub.

Somewhere in the haze of that year, the realisation that our weekend routine of all-night drug taking is taking its toll on me begins to emerge. The initial come down happens right after the drug wears off and it only abates after a little sleep, which isn't at all easy. This low, however, is short-lived. Every Tuesday, I experience a come down I can only describe as a kind of temporary depression. It lasts all day. Then, from Wednesday, we're on the countdown again to Friday night.

Occasionally, we pull a two-nighter and go clubbing on both Friday *and* Saturday night. However, this is only over a bank holiday weekend, and the week that follows those weekends is really horrible. I often ask myself why I'm treating my body and my mind so badly, and instinctively, I know it will all come to an end very soon.

'I can't be bothered to dress up tonight,' I say to Penny over the phone.

'Me neither,' she replies, stifling a yawn. 'I'll call Tiffany and tell her. And I'm not going to wear any makeup tonight either.'

That night, we all wear jeans and trainers to the club, with absolutely no makeup at all. The only reason we're in the club is to take Ecstasy and, to a lesser degree, to dance.

It's four in the morning. I'm looking around and I realise I'm no longer having fun.

It isn't easy, but the following weekend, I make the decision to stay at home. Tiffany and Penny go out without me. I feel really *terrible*. Friday night takes a week to pass and there is a physical wrenching inside my guts all night. I can't sleep. I want to jump in the car and drive up to London to join them, even at five in the morning. But I don't.

It's the end of my love-in-a-pill days.

In some ways it's easy for me to stay out of the club because José doesn't take drugs and he isn't into the club scene at all. Despite that, I feel alone and depressed during this empty phase of my life. I've left the high of the club behind me, but I feel frustrated when I spend time with José, because I desperately want a more intimate relationship with him. However, I'm simply too frightened to take the risk, both physically and emotionally. I'm stuck, and there seems to be very little for me to feel happy about. Work is monotonous and the days stretch out endlessly. I really need something to pick me up, and for the first time in years, I find myself yearning for Barbados. I miss the beach, the slow pace of life and the glorious west coast sunsets. Ironically, they're almost all the reasons why I left.

Robyn is single again and she seems to be around a lot more, which I'm grateful for. I ask her if she's interested in joining me for a holiday in Barbados, and before I've even finished my sentence, she's already said 'yes'. I also ask José.

'Can Jack come too?' he replies. Jack is José's best friend and they live together. 'He can keep Robyn company, eh?' He laughs, winking. Jack is also a member of the strip troupe and I've got to know him quite well over the past year. I think it's a great idea.

'Sure, why not?' I reply. Secretly, I'm pleased.

There is one thing, however, which is bothering me. It's been gnawing away at the back of my mind for quite some time. I haven't seen my mother, or even spoken to her, in several years. Not since leaving Barbados. My conscience often tells me to call or write to her, but almost immediately, I remember the terrible occasion when she bit a chunk out of my arm and very quickly, I change my mind. I often wonder if she's mellowed over the years. I hope she has, because I realise I'm finally ready to make my peace with her. I'm certainly willing to take a chance, despite everything that's happened in the past. Right then, I make the impossible decision to see her during my holiday.

CHAPTER 10

Robyn and I walk into my father's upstairs apartment and put our bags down. I'm already hot and sweaty and I'm desperate for a pee. The phone rings. It's José. He's been on the island with Jack for three days already and he seems eager to see me. That makes me feel good.

'Come over, Rach. You have *got* to see this place!' he shouts, excited. I've managed to find them a small apartment only a short drive down the coast and I'm keen to see it for myself. Robyn and I are staying with my father, which means that we can afford to rent a car. The buses in Barbados are not for the faint-hearted and I'm grateful for the small Suzuki we picked up at the airport.

Fifteen minutes later, we pull into where José and Jack are staying. Their apartment is set within lush, tropical gardens. There are several mature palm trees and a prolifically flowering hibiscus shrub, which surrounds their single-storey villa. Inside, there are two single beds, an en-suite bathroom and a very small kitchenette. Despite the rather diminutive size of their accommodation, they are both very pleased with it. There is also a larger communal building next to the parking area with a restaurant which, José tells me, serves a Bajan buffet dinner on a Thursday evening.

We decide not to go very far that first night, as Robyn and I are both tired from the long flight. There's a beach bar a short drive down the coast, which I know well. When we arrive, Jack and José go straight up to the bar and order four rum punches. Meanwhile, Robyn and I find an empty table and we both sit down facing the sea.

I haven't allowed myself any headspace in recent weeks to think about this holiday. It suddenly dawns on me that I'm actually back in Barbados, it's January, I'm in shorts and José is here with me.

I take a long, deep breath. My shoulders drop. I tilt my neck from side to side to relieve the tight muscles. It pops on the left side and the tension I've been holding onto for days, evaporates. I'm floating.

Less than fifty yards away, a wave pulls back, rolls and then breaks on the pale white sand. It rides a little way up the beach towards us, spreading slowly upwards before retreating once more. The sound is soft. Gentle. Behind me, calypso is playing on the radio. I want to devour the tranquillity. I turn to Robyn with a smile.

'How lovely is this?' I say.

'Pure bloody paradise, Rach,' Robyn replies, winking towards the boys over at the bar. Her meaning is not lost on me and I've already noticed the glances between Jack and Robyn. They seem to be getting on like a house on fire. The boys join us with drinks and a menu and the four of us are silent for a few moments as we decide what to eat.

Soon, the barman is bringing over four plates of flying fish sandwiches. Bajan seasoning drifts fleetingly under my nose, making my mouth water as he puts the plates down on the table in front of us. I've missed this smell and savour the sweet-and-sour taste of my rum punch with its dusting of nutmeg.

The sun sinks silently on the horizon, the firmament alight with streaks of gold and crimson against a velvet sky. Puffs of white clouds, their bellies ablaze with fire, drift together. This isn't a time for words.

Silence.

I stifle a yawn. Robyn does the same. José and Jack have already acclimatised, but Robyn and I are fading fast.

Before we call it a night, we return to my father's apartment for a quick nightcap so I can introduce my father to the boys.

Dad is the perfect host. He makes José and Jack feel very welcome. He also makes them laugh. A lot. When we finish our drinks, Robyn says goodnight and trots off to bed. I offer to drop the boys back at their apartment.

I return feeling upbeat, only to find my father standing at the top of the stairs with a face like thunder. He's obviously been waiting for my return. His hands are on his hips and I can tell that he's angry about something. I'm taken aback.

'What's wrong, Dad?' I ask.

'Rachel, I'm very happy for you and Robyn to stay here, but you can't just bring anyone back, whenever you want. You really put me on the spot tonight. You didn't even check with me first. Rachel, this is my house. My *home!*' he shouts, growing red in the face.

I don't recognise this version of my father. I'm dumbfounded. My father is absolutely furious. This is the very first time I've *ever* heard him speaking out and suddenly, I feel very small.

'I-I'm really sorry, Dad,' I mumble, walking past him with my head down. I slink off to bed.

He's finally found his voice.

I lie wide awake in bed that night, feeling overwhelmed with guilt for misreading the situation. It's been over six years since my father and I have lived under the same roof and it was never a problem before for me to bring friends home. Dad always loved company and a lively atmosphere, and I took it for granted he would be happy to meet the boys. Clearly, he was putting on a front tonight and that makes me feel terrible. I can't work out if he's angry with me because he can see how much I like José, and he doesn't approve, or if perhaps he feels threatened by the presence of two young, virile males. Whatever the reason, I make the decision not to bring José or Jack back to my father's apartment again. Eventually, I manage to drift into a fitful sleep to the sound of Robyn's loud snores.

The following day, Robyn and I are up early. We decide not to call the boys but instead, we take a drive down to a beach a little further along the coast. I'm quiet for most of the morning and Robyn eventually asks me what's on my mind.

'Oh, it's nothing,' I lie. 'I'm just a bit tired.'

Now that José and Jack are here in Barbados, I realise how unhappy I am with the status quo. I want to be more than José's "friend" and I regret being so adamant about having a platonic friendship with him back in England.

Call it the sun, sea, or perhaps the rum, but my resolve is wavering, and I'm wondering how I can let him know without making a complete and utter fool of myself. I don't want to tell Robyn any of this, because I've always denied how I really feel about José. Not that she believes me. Who would? He's gorgeous! That infuriates me but only because it's true. Eventually, Robyn's voice cuts through my thoughts.

'I wonder if the boys have tried to call us yet?' she muses. I look up at her sharply. *Is she reading my mind?* I must look guilty because she immediately asks me what's wrong. I think better of lying to her again; instead, I take a deep breath and come clean.

'I want to tell José I like him,' I say flatly. 'As more than a friend, I mean.' I feel a little ridiculous saying that out loud.

'Well *of course* you do, Rach.' She laughs. 'You always have. That's *obvious*. So, why now?' She looks at me curiously.

'Well, I-I just don't want to resist him anymore.' Now it's my turn to laugh, but I'm not amused. 'It's bloody hard work.'

Robyn looks over at me, serious for a moment. 'Then don't. I mean don't resist him, Rach. You've done that for ages. So, what will you do?'

'I have absolutely no idea. None whatsoever,' I reply, feeling deflated. I still have concerns about whether it's wise to tell him, but I just want to be true to myself — to hell with the consequences.

When we get back that afternoon, there are two messages from José on my father's answering machine. My heart does a somersault. *Two!* José is wondering where I am and he wants me to call back. I look up at Robyn, who's also standing in the room, listening. She's now grinning from ear to ear. I notice she's caught the sun already. Her nose is pink.

'Best ring him back then, eh?' She winks at me. I feel nervous but I'm relieved when José picks up after the first ring.

'Rachel, where the bloody hell have you been?' he says.

I relax instantly. 'We thought we'd leave you two to sleep in as we were both up before six,' I reply. The real truth is I wanted to remain a little aloof, rather than rushing over there first thing. But I keep that to myself. We chat for a while longer and arrange to meet up for sundowners. Robyn and I shower, change and leave my father's apartment in a cloud of perfume.

When we arrive, José comes running over to the car with a huge smile on his face.

'Hello! *Wow!*' He whistles at us as he gets in. 'Jack is just locking up. We *love* it here! Thanks for inviting us, Rach.' He pats me on the shoulder. Even that innocent touch makes my heart miss a beat. He's now sitting directly behind me. I'm very aware of him and inside I'm bursting, but outwardly I'm my normal, calm self.

'I'm glad you like it,' is all I trust myself to say, and then Jack comes swaggering over and gets in the back of the car. He echoes José's sentiments and we set off for the beach bar.

We've been at the beach bar for over an hour and I'm on my third rum punch. I haven't eaten a thing since breakfast and I'm tipsy. I suggest we order something to eat before I do a Bridget Jones and embarrass myself in front of José. I'm still hoping for the opportunity to talk to him later.

We order flying fish sandwiches again and yet another round of drinks. I'm not sure if another drink is a very good idea and I'm relieved to have something to eat when it finally arrives. I'm a little less squiffy after that.

Later that evening, I get in the car pretty damn drunk and I drive us all back to the boys' apartment. *Not cool, Rachel.* We arrive safely and, as the Universe would have it, the ideal opportunity for me to speak to José finally presents itself. He suggests we go and sit under a palm tree in a more secluded part of the garden while Robyn and Jack go back to the boys' apartment for a nightcap. *Ahem.*

José pats the grass and invites me to sit down next to him, which I do a little clumsily. I kick off my shoes and lean back against the tree, listening to the whistling frogs nearby. It's such a beautiful sound, very tropical. I take a deep breath and close my eyes, which is not a very good idea. My head is spinning. I feel as if I've just stepped off a Waltzer. I open my eyes again. *Fast.*

José is as charming as ever. He speaks about his childhood and growing up in northern Spain. As he speaks, all I can think about is his mouth. I become fixated on it. I'm also thinking I need to sober up a little. We talk some more, but I can't focus on what he's saying. After almost a year of resisting him, I am ready to erupt. My ability to suppress my feelings is crumbling away with each passing second.

'José,' I slur. 'Kiss me.' I lean towards him and he stops mid-sentence, looking at me as if I've just slapped him with a wet fish.

'*What?*' He continues to look at me strangely. I take a deep breath and repeat myself, with a lot less conviction this time.

Dear God, he thinks I've lost the plot.

Flushed with embarrassment, I quickly mumble an apology and attempt to pick up my shoes, ready to make a hasty exit.

'Rachel?' He grabs my arm and pulls me back down onto the grass with a bump. My head swims. I suddenly feel like crying and want to be anywhere else but sitting in this beautiful tropical garden with a musclebound stripper who is looking at me like I'm quite mad. Perhaps I am.

'I-I'm sorry, José. I don't know what came over me. S-sorry.' I look up at him again. My eyes are filling with tears, but before I can say any more, he leans over and kisses me deeply.

He takes my breath away.

I try to speak again but he won't let me. He lays me down on the grass and all those months of wanting to be close to him melt away as we lose ourselves in each other. I'm completely overwhelmed with an urgency and tenderness for him. It's a heady mix I've never before experienced. We know each other well enough, but knowing him in such an intimate way is totally new, and yet reassuringly familiar at the same time. Any fear I had of being rejected disappears instantly and I let go and relax with him.

I know I've taken him by surprise, not simply by asking him to kiss me, but by showing him my entirely uninhibited side. For just one brief moment, I've stepped into his world and it has caught him off guard. A small triumph for allowing myself to be added to all those notches on his bedpost. Although this notch is being carved into a palm tree which, I think, is *far* more interesting.

'We'd better check on Robyn and Jack,' he eventually whispers to me. I've fallen asleep in his arms. *Delicious*. I slowly become aware of my surroundings and wonder how long we've been in the garden. I'd floated off to a lovely place somewhere far, far away, and totally lost track of time. Cloud nine, I suppose it was.

'Yes, ok,' I reply sleepily, looking around for my clothes. We dress and make our way through the gardens to their apartment. José opens the door gingerly, not wanting to interrupt anything that may be going on inside. However, he needn't have worried. They are both fast asleep on Jack's single bed and Robyn is snoring loudly. José looks over to me and bursts out laughing.

'Bloody hell, Rach. She's inhaling the room!'

This sets me off, too, which wakes them both up.

'W-what happened?' Robyn says huskily, disorientated, as she tries to shake the sleep out of her head. She seems alarmed. José and I look at each other again and that's it. We fall about laughing, no longer concerned about the noise we're making. We just can't help it. We are literally crying with laughter, and the more confused Robyn is, the more we howl. Eventually, we manage to calm down, in between small bursts of the giggles. Jack has one eye open. He's been laughing along with us, although he hasn't got a clue what he's laughing at. It's contagious, I suppose, but Robyn is not at all impressed.

'I'll tell you in the car,' I say to her quickly, trying not to laugh again. 'We'd better go, Rob. The sun will be up soon!'

I plant a lingering kiss on José's mouth and with that, we bid the boys goodnight. Robyn speaks as soon as the car door is closed.

'It looks like things worked out for you and José.' She is referring to our parting kiss. 'And *what the hell* were you all laughing about?' She shouts but she doesn't seem angry anymore. Robyn is not a morning person. I know that well enough.

'You were snoring, Rob, and yes, I had an amazing night.' I look over at her with a huge smile on my face. She grins back and then she laughs.

'Good for you, Rach.' She leans over and pats my leg.

We discuss our evening as I drive the short distance home. We've both been triumphant. I wonder to myself if this is how boys feel when they're on holiday in a similar situation, having scored. It's liberating.

I could get used to this, I think to myself, smugly.

CHAPTER 11

Robyn leaves a few days later.

I see her off at the airport and am very sad to see her go. We've both had such a fantastic time together, but she needs to get back to work. I still have another three weeks left on the island, but at least the boys will be with me a little while longer.

Over the next twenty-four hours, José and Jack come up with the idea of performing a one-off strip show in one of the local nightclubs before returning home. Despite knowing how much Bajans love a good party, I'm not so keen on the idea. West Indian dancing can be just as suggestive, but the difference in Barbados is, there is always *something*, even the slimmest sliver of material, to cover a dancer's modesty out in public — even at *Kadooment*, where everyone lets their hair down to celebrate the end of the sugar cane harvest.

José and Jack take *everything* off when they perform back in England. Nothing at all is left to the imagination. If they really do want to perform in Barbados, I suggest that they, at least, keep their underwear on. They look at each other with a mischievous twinkle in their eyes and immediately set to work finding a suitable venue.

Within a week, they've secured a popular club on the south coast of the island in an area, ironically, called 'the strip'.

They create a raunchy new routine and, with the help of the local radio station advertising a 'sensational, once-in-a-lifetime ladies' night,' every last ticket for their performance is sold out. The boys are absolutely delighted with the response. They're due to perform on their very last night on the island and we all agree it's a great way to end their holiday.

They rehearse their new routine each morning and we meet down at the beach during the afternoons. I drive over to watch them practising one morning and am really impressed with their performance. It's lively, sexy and more than a little cheeky. I feel certain the women will love it. However, I remind the boys about the importance of leaving their underwear on so as not to offend the locals. This matter is reiterated in a phone call to the club the night before the show. A high-ranking policeman has heard about the boys' performance on the radio and he calls to speak to the manager to remind him about the public exposure laws in Barbados. Apparently, the policeman is very clear: José and Jack will be arrested if they strip naked in public. The manager assures him that this will not happen.

While all of this is going on, José and I have found an easy way to be with each other. It's very different from the way we were together in England. Now, we kiss each other on the mouth and when we are together, we hold hands, like lovers. Oddly though, we haven't had any time alone since our night in the garden and I feel reluctant to speak to José about it.

On the night of the show, the very last day of the boys' holiday, I drop them off early and promise to be back in plenty of time to watch their performance. When I return a few hours later, the club is full to the rafters with well-dressed women, coiffed and perfumed for their night out. I feel more than a little self-conscious as I move through the crowd to take the seat that has been reserved for me in the middle of the front row. Despite the fact that I've seen the boys perform several times before, I begin to feel nervous. Thankfully, it isn't very long before the music in the club stops and José appears at the front of the stage with a microphone. A sharp, high-pitched whine feeds back from the speakers before settling into a low hum and then disappearing altogether. This only heightens my nerves as the entire venue has stopped dead and everyone is staring at José. However, he isn't the least bit fazed by the sound-check failure. José is smiling confidently at the audience. In fact, he seems to be relishing the instant attention.

'Well, *hel-lo* all you gorgeous Bar-bajan beauties!' he shouts out, followed by a wink. Well, that's it. The response from the women is both overwhelming and deafening. They scream their approval and José laughs, clearly pleased with their response. He speaks a little about what's to come and then he hands his microphone to a passing waiter as their music begins. I recognise their opening number immediately. Jack appears from the back of the stage and is greeted with an equally rapturous response.

Their routine is flawless and everyone in the club is on their feet, clapping and screaming. Jack and José have now stripped down to their canary-yellow thongs and they are thrusting and gyrating at the crowd. The women are chanting in unison: 'Off, off, off,' as the boys continue to tease them relentlessly.

'What do you want?' José shouts playfully, cupping a hand behind one of his ears.

'Off, off, *off!*' they all scream again at the tops of their voices. José and Jack look at each other knowingly and before you can say 'lunchbox,' they've whipped off the last piece of their clothing and they're standing naked and semi-erect in front of the crowd.

Now, it always amazed me that José managed to perform naked, effectively with an erection. Initially, I assumed he was aroused by all the attention. However, I will let you in on a little trade secret here, as I found it so interesting. José explained to me that before every performance, it's normal for male strippers to disappear into a nearby bathroom, with a sexy magazine if necessary, and when they've managed to achieve a satisfactory level of 'erect,' they tie a rubber band around the base of their most private, and soon to be very public, part, thus maintaining optimum size for the duration of their performance. It makes perfect sense. Gyrating away flaccid would not have quite the same appeal.

I instantly think about the police caution and I look behind me to the back of the room to see if I can spot anyone in uniform making their way to the front of the club, but I can't see a thing. The women are all on their feet, screaming and clapping, and the noise is beginning to hurt my ears. José and Jack bow, wave, and in the very next moment they disappear off the back of the stage.

The lights come up in the rest of the club and the music begins again. The women slowly disperse. Several make their way to the bar, but I sit in my seat in the front row on my own, not really knowing where to go or what to do. My mind is working overtime. *Why did the boys defy the police warning and take everything off? Will they be in trouble?* No one is taking a blind bit of notice. Or so it seems.

Soon enough, Jack and José appear, smiling broadly and clearly buzzing from the response of the women. Once they finish chatting with the manager, who seems delighted with the turn-out, we all leave. I remain subdued.

'What's up, Rach?' José asks as I pull out of a parking space a little way down the road from the club. He's just finished counting out a large amount of cash, which the manager handed over in a brown envelope.

'You weren't supposed to take everything off, José.' I feel a little ridiculous saying that out loud to a professional stripper.

'It's fine, Rach,' Jack pipes up from the back. 'They *loved* it!' he adds dismissively.

I'm not really in the mood to talk, and perhaps the truth of the matter is, a part of me feels strange witnessing the crazed response of all the women now that José and I are together as a couple. I haven't really considered what it would actually feel like to be José's girlfriend, knowing what he does for a living. I've avoided it for so long. I don't like the way I feel at all. It isn't jealousy. The overwhelming emotion I am feeling is *shame*. I'm embarrassed knowing my boyfriend exposes himself for a living.

José and Jack chat excitedly all the way back to their apartment, oblivious to my thoughts. I remain silent, but my mind continues to work overtime. Tomorrow, the boys will fly home and I'll be left on my own. Is this a holiday romance as far as José's concerned? Is this a holiday romance as far as *I'm* concerned? I really don't know if I want to be José's girlfriend. The reality of the evening and the high I've been riding all holiday comes to an abrupt end. I suppose you could say I came down to earth with a bump. Right there in the car.

We arrive back at the boys' apartment and I stay seated in the car with the engine running.

'Aren't you coming in, Rach? It's our last night,' José says, cocking his head on one side. I know he wants me to stay, but my head is all over the place, and I'm not sure what to do.

'I'm n-not feeling so good,' I reply, not entirely lying. 'I really want to go home and sleep, José,' I add truthfully. 'Can we catch up tomorrow?'

He agrees and leans in to kiss me, but I turn my head and offer him my cheek instead. He looks at me quizzically but he doesn't linger in the car. Jack has already left us with a brief, 'Laters!' before heading back to the apartment. José waves to me in the headlights as I reverse out of the drive. I feel like crying, but I only allow the tears to flow when I'm finally in bed. It dawns on me how much I like José and how much I will miss him. I'm also aware that we've never actually spoken about our relationship or whether we'll continue seeing each other as a couple when we return to England. Eventually, with my mind swinging from hope to doubt and then back again, I fall into an exhausted sleep.

My father wakes me up the following morning, leaning on the doorway of my bedroom. He's been saying something to me.

'W-what?' I say sleepily. My eyes are still puffy from crying and I have a terrible headache.

'José is on the phone,' he says again. 'Do you want to take it or call him back?'

I groan, remembering my turmoil the previous night.

'I'll call him back please, Dad.' I say eventually, pulling myself up to a sitting position. My mind starts turning over again. I jump out of bed and head straight to the shower. I let the cool water wash over me for a long time. It feels good, and by the time I'm dressed, my father has made me a cup of tea and is waiting for me in the kitchen. He knows me well enough to recognise I'm unhappy, but he also knows me well enough to recognise that I don't want to talk about it. I sit down and sip my tea, looking anywhere else but at him. Eventually, I speak.

'The boys are leaving today, Dad, and I'm not sure how I feel about it,' is all I say.

'Would you like a fried egg, darling?' he replies gently.

I smile up at him. 'I'd really love that. Thanks, Dad.'

After breakfast, I call José back and arrange to meet him and Jack down at the beach. Their flight isn't due to leave until much later that evening, which means we can spend the whole day together.

The weather is perfect and I do my very best not to think about the status quo between José and me. In the meantime, I make sure we enjoy our last day together.

The day passes much too quickly, however, and before long we're on the highway heading south towards the airport, with me trying my level best not to be glum. I know Jack and José have both really enjoyed their time on the island and I'm pleased to have been a part of it.

I give Jack a squeeze before he walks through customs. José and I have a long, lingering kiss.

'Thanks babe. See you in a fortnight,' he says, pinching the end of my nose affectionately, before following Jack into the customs hall. A huge lump has now formed in my throat as I wave goodbye through the large glass partition. José smiles back at me and then disappears into the crowd.

My legs have turned to lead as I walk back towards the car. I realise I need some change for the car park and so I stop at a small café to buy a bottle of water. When I leave the café, however, I notice a small skirmish on the far side of the airport, just outside the arrivals hall. There are a group of policemen leading two men swiftly towards a police van.

'Oh, my God!' I shout in surprise. *It's José and Jack!* I'm now in a panic. I run over towards them, but the police van pulls away with them in the back before I can reach them. I don't know what to do. I run to the car and drive back to my father's house at breakneck speed, with my stomach in knots. I know the boys have been arrested because of the previous night.

So, they didn't get away with it. Where are they being taken?

I desperately want to know what's happened to them. Thankfully, I don't need to wait very long to find out. As soon as I walk through the door, my father hands me the phone. His face is very serious.

'It's José,' he says to me as I quickly grab the phone out of his hands and walk away. My heart is beating ten to the dozen.

'José! What on earth is going on?' My legs feel wobbly and so I sit on the floor while he tells me everything.

Once they passed through customs, José and Jack were approached by several policemen who arrested them for exposing themselves during their performance at the club the previous night. They were immediately put into handcuffs and driven from the airport to the main police station in Bridgetown where, José tells me, they will be kept in a police cell overnight.

I hear no concern *at all* in José's voice. In fact, he seems to be finding the entire business amusing. Suddenly, my ears feel hot and I begin to bristle.

Doesn't he recognise the seriousness of the situation? Doesn't he care?

I keep my feelings to myself and try, instead, to listen to what he's saying. They are both due to appear in court the following morning and he feels confident they will be let off lightly. The policemen are treating them very well and, apparently, the atmosphere in the police station is light and jovial. Before he says goodbye, José tells me not to worry. He's convinced that everything will be ok.

I, on the other hand, am not happy at all. I am fuming.

The next morning, José and Jack are taken to the magistrates' court and I make sure that I'm there to support them. They are both fined heavily – all their cash earnings – and told to leave Barbados on the next available flight. This seems ironic as the police took them *off* their flight the night before. They are also banned from the island permanently. Really, they've got off lightly, but I'm absolutely gutted about the ban and there's no opportunity for me to speak to José before he and Jack are taken away again.

I return home like a burst balloon. A twice-burst balloon. I make myself a strong coffee and I wait near my father's phone for a call from José. I wait for the entire day. *Silence*. I stare at the phone a lot. It mocks me by remaining deathly quiet.

I've given up completely on receiving a call when suddenly, the phone rings. It makes me jump. I leap up to answer it, but it's not José. It's a friend of mine, letting me know that José and Jack were spotted earlier at the airport, boarding a plane. They've gone.

I'm completely and utterly exhausted with all the drama of the previous twenty-four hours. I pour myself a stiff rum and sit outside on my father's balcony, listening to the whistling frogs in the dark. I stay there for quite some time, not really knowing what to think. My eyelids are beginning to feel heavy and I decide to go to bed.

José calls me just before seven the following morning and apologises for not speaking to me sooner. I'm not quite awake and he's talking very quickly. He's now very upset that he's been banned from the island. However, he tells me that neither he nor Jack regret their decision to do the show, nor do they regret their decision to take everything off in the club. I think it's *this* part that makes me feel very angry with him once again. Not least because I'd warned them both about it and they'd blatantly ignored me. I'm still very tired and I just want to get off the phone. It's ridiculous really, given the torture I'd felt the day before, desperate to hear José's voice.

'Let's talk about it when I'm back, eh?' I say wearily.

'Sure. Yes, ok, Rach.' We say goodbye and I drag myself to the kitchen to make a cup of tea.

That afternoon, I drop into the local supermarket to pick up a few things for supper. At the very front of the shop, as I'm walking in, I notice a stack of newspapers with a huge colour photograph of José and Jack plastered all over the front page. I gasp.

So, they are now minor celebrities!

I pick one up and add it to my basket, a little self-consciously. José's face is staring up at me the entire way around the supermarket. The photograph has been taken outside the courtroom. It looks a little distorted in my shopping basket – José appears to be winking at me. I am in an alternate universe.

As soon as I get home, I read the article from start to finish. It's not at all uncomplimentary. It depicts the boys as cheeky and foolish rather than painting them as criminals. I'm relieved. I fold away the newspaper and put it in the bottom of my empty suitcase to show José and Jack when I return.

Strangely, the feeling of sadness that has been with me for two days lifts as soon as I zip the case closed. Perhaps it's not so bad having a couple of weeks to myself. I take a long, deep breath and I stretch like a cat. I fancy a swim and so I head down to the beach, alone.

Before I leave the island, I discover something very interesting. I'm told that the wife of a high-ranking policeman also attended the club to watch the boys' performance, and apparently, she enjoyed the show just a little *too* much. I laugh when I hear this. I wonder if it might be the wife of the very same policeman who'd called the club with the warning?

My amusement soon dissipates as my mind turns to my mother. I made a promise to myself that I'd make contact with her as soon as the boys returned to England. Speaking to her is the very last thing I feel like doing. However, I know I'll only feel guilty if I don't arrange to see her before I go. I take a deep breath, pick up the phone and dial her number.

'Rachel, is that you? Are you *here* in Barbados?' she says excitedly. My stomach contracts immediately. I haven't heard her voice in years and my heart begins to beat rapidly as she proceeds to talk *at* me, ten to the dozen. Tactfully, I manage to deflect most of her questions by promising to pay her a visit the following afternoon. The very brief exchange has left me feeling slightly nauseous and the feeling stays with me right up until I pull up outside her flat the next day. With every fibre in my body wanting to stay in the relative safety of the car, I get out and walk up the two flights of stairs to her front door. I pause for a brief moment to compose myself, take a deep breath and knock loudly.

'*Rachel!*' my mother cries, as she flings the door open to her tiny flat. She attempts to embrace me, but I remain stiff and upright with my arms stuck to my sides. I step inside and have a cursory look around. Mum now lives on the south coast of the island, above a video shop. It's a far cry from the luxury of our west coast home. The air inside the flat is hot and humid, and the fan that oscillates noisily in the corner of her sitting room does little to cool the small space.

I sit down, overcome with a growing sense of claustrophobia. My knees are trembling slightly. Not an altogether unfamiliar feeling in such close proximity to my mother. Fight Flight. *Freeze*. She always had this effect on me and nothing has changed. Tiny beads of sweat are now breaking out above my top lip and I'm beginning to have second thoughts about coming.

'How have you been?' Mum asks eagerly. 'I've often wondered, you know.'

Now *that* suddenly makes me feel angry. It flashes through me from the centre of my chest, down my arms to my fingertips. I feel a little more in control, which, I suppose, is better than feeling scared. I immediately want to ask her why she never made any attempt to write, but I think better of going backwards. *In all fairness, neither did I.* With good reason, I quickly remind myself. My emotions are all over the place. I take another deep breath.

'I've been ok, Mum. Getting on with life,' I concede. With that, a very large elephant enters the room and sits down heavily on the floor in front of me. I do my very best to ignore it. It just won't do to bring up the past. Not now. *Not ever.* This is a new start, of sorts. The elephant cocks his head to one side and raises an eyebrow at me in disbelief.

For the next two hours, we make utterly ridiculous small talk in the oppressive heat of my mother's flat and a reluctant truce is called, without me venturing into the past. I feel awkward for almost the entire time, although I relax a fraction observing Mum's valiant effort to make the peace. It's peculiar seeing her like this.

I leave with the elephant, feeling lighter than I've done in years. I'm glad I've made the effort to contact her, although I won't go as far as saying that I want or expect to have any kind of "normal" relationship with her. I'm still extremely wary of her, but at least we're now talking, and this feels infinitely better.

That night, back at my father's house, I sleep deeper and longer than I've done in as long as I can remember.

I only see my mother once more, at the very end of the holiday when she turns up at the airport to say goodbye.

Oddly, she would always insist on being at the airport whenever we were travelling back to boarding school. It seemed very important to her. To this day, I'm not entirely sure why. She never once wrote when we were away at school, but she would always make the effort to go to the airport whenever we were leaving. Perhaps, like me, she relished that delicious feeling of freedom after we'd left.

When I'm leaving this time, I feel overcome with sadness. We embrace and she smells of Elnett and Daz. Suddenly, she seems much younger to me, like a sister or a friend, and in that precise moment, I get a sense of her... not as my mother with all our terrible history, but of *her*; Carmen Lincoln, a young girl with her very own history. It's a very peculiar feeling – as if I am seeing behind the barrier for the very first time.

CHAPTER 12

I look out of the window at the dull grey mizzle of the
English countryside, which is finally appearing as we descend
out of the thick cloud on our approach into Gatwick Airport.

'Oh, joy,' I mutter under my breath. What a fine morning
to be arriving back from paradise. *Not.* The weather reflects my
spirits entirely. I am utterly depressed to be back in England
again after such a wonderful few weeks away in the sun.

Robyn is there to meet me and she talks non-stop, as usual,
all the way back to her place. She suggests I have a kip as she
drops me off outside her front door before setting off again for
work. I've arranged to stay with Robyn until I can find myself
a place to rent, but I feel very lonely and depressed as I walk
inside alone. I have no job, no fixed abode, and probably no
boyfriend. I also have a rather strong sense of déjà vu.

Nothing in my life feels solid and the harsh reality of my
situation, and all the uncertainty, hits me like a ton of bricks.
I delay calling José for a few days. First, I want to acclimatise.
He's written me one letter since leaving Barbados, but we've
not spoken again on the phone. His letter was very sweet,
but there was no mention of the future or how he feels about
me. I desperately want to hear his voice again and to have
his reassurance that our time together was not just a holiday

romance. However, as the days pass, I feel a terrible sense of foreboding. Eventually, I pluck up the courage to call him. My heart is beating wildly inside my chest as I wait for him to pick up.

'Rach!' he shouts down the line, 'you're back.' My heart skips a beat. The relief I feel is palpable when he immediately asks if he can come and see me. He is knocking on Robyn's front door in less than two hours, and minutes later we're making love on the bedroom carpet upstairs. Opening up old wounds, quite literally, on my lower back.

'I've really missed you, babe,' he says as I nestle against him. I feel safe and, for the first time in several days, I feel happy. Everything is going to be ok. *Or is it?*

The next morning, José kisses me and leaves early to return to London. He has a show to rehearse for and he's meeting Jack and the others later that day. He assures me he'll call, but there's been no mention at all about the future or about *us*.

I stay in bed, looking up at the ceiling, wondering what the hell I am going to do with my life. I still haven't plucked up the courage to ask José if we're officially an item. On one hand, I feel reassured that he came straight over to see me. On the other, I fear I'm just another notch, especially as the days pass and I hear absolutely nothing more from him.

I almost call him several times but then I think better of it. *Be cool, Rach.* I feel anything but. The reality that our relationship is nothing more than a holiday romance slowly begins to dawn on me.

Eventually, José does call, but the line is really bad and he seems distracted. He's been doing a run of shows from Edinburgh to Bristol and he won't be back in London for another week. He promises to call me then. After I put the phone down, I begin to think about all those screaming women, up and down the country, waving their backstage passes, and I feel miserable. I've been back less than a fortnight and I already know I don't want the unconventional life of being a professional stripper's girlfriend. *What on earth led me to believe this could ever work?*

Lust... and all that godforsaken rum.

However, I am not, nor will I ever be, one to drag my heels for very long. I think long and hard about my options. I once dreamed about being a model. Perhaps every girl does. Silly, maybe, but I'm lying in bed that morning envisioning a glamorous life, jet-setting off to stunning locations all over the world, gracing the pages of glossy magazines. *Am I thin enough? Am I pretty enough? Can I make a living out of it?... Just go for it, Rach! What have you got to lose?*

What are you trying to prove? I think to myself in earnest.

And so, over the following few weeks, I put together a portfolio of photographs with the help of a friend who also happens to be a budding photographer. I have a black-and-white model card made up with the best photographs from my portfolio, and I send them to various agencies around the country. Then, I wait. And I wait.

Nothing happens for weeks until I finally receive a call from an agency that supplies models for promotional work. They want me to work at the motor show with another twenty girls. *Why not?*

First, we're taught about the latest model of Rover cars at the Rover headquarters in Slough. This is my first experience of turning heads as we file through the office en masse. After our day's training, we are each given a red uniform and a ridiculous pair of red high heels. Then we're all sent off to the National Exhibition Centre in Birmingham for a fortnight. Not quite the jet-set life I've envisioned, to be honest. However, I accept the job because I'm broke and already up to my eyeballs in debt.

It's probably one of the worst experiences of my life. We spend ten hours a day on our feet in the stifling, windowless indoor arena, which is packed full of people and many thousands of brightly polished cars. We spend the majority of our time fending off motor enthusiasts who have halitosis. We smile sweetly at them as we take down their details so that local dealers up and down the country can call them back for a test drive. The cars are nice enough, but our feet are in agony at the end of every single shift. We look anything *but* glamorous walking back to our hotel at the end of each day – as if we have rubber ankle bones.

The only thing that makes the entire experience bearable is flirting outrageously with an Irish car cleaner called Paddy. He is six foot two, drop-dead gorgeous and I like his aftershave. He stops to chat to me every time he comes around to polish all the cars on the Rover stand.

Up yours, José. Two can play that game.

Promotion work very soon becomes my bread and butter. Sometimes I have to wait for up to three months to be paid, but eventually my money comes through. I even manage to do a small amount of bona fide modelling work through a new agency, in-store modelling at an evening wear wholesaler in London.

It's there I meet Annie – a blonde version of me with a very similar sense of humour. We spend hours together in little more than a windowless cupboard as the salesmen thrust dress after sequinned dress through the door for us to try on. Then we parade around the shop floor for fashion buyers, encouraging them to purchase the dresses. It's quite a skill, looking aloof and glamorous in between heavy bouts of giggling in our hot little cupboard.

Through Annie, I find much more modelling work. This time, I'm on the catwalk. I am now part of a theatrical runway show for a successful bridalwear company. The work is well paid and I love it. All the girls in the show soon become friends as we travel to different venues across the country. Finally, I am beginning to enjoy life again.

And José? Well, he never did ring me back.

And then, I meet Alex.

I'm walking up the stone path to the entrance of our local pub when I first notice him. He's sitting on a wall outside, talking to some of his friends. Our eyes lock and, like every good or perhaps trashy novel professes, I feel the electricity between us *instantaneously*. I am captivated by his piercing blue-grey eyes and I make sure we are introduced that evening.

'Hi, Rach,' Alex drawls. He extends a large hand and grasps one of mine. He has a strong grip. I like that.

'H-hi,' I reply, smiling back at him. I am feeling a little overwhelmed by the sheer size of him. He is six foot four inches of towering muscle.

'Fancy a game of pool?' he asks casually. It's an excellent idea, as I could do with some kind of a distraction to tone down the intensity.

'Sounds like fun.' I accept quickly, smiling up at him with a little more conviction this time. We make our way through the smoke and hubbub of the packed bar to the pool room at the very back of the pub. It's much quieter in here.

Alex and I play pool and chat to each other like old friends meeting up after a very long absence. I find him charming in a gentle and unassuming way. He has an aura of quiet strength around him, which slowly draws me in as I circle the pool table. All the while, I pretend to concentrate on the position of the balls.

By the time one of the barmaids pokes her head through the door and calls 'last orders', I am completely smitten. After three large glasses of red, I am also a little tipsy and this gives me the courage to ask him out.

'Fancy meeting up again?' I ask, through lowered lashes.

'I'm sorry, Rach, I'm off to the Alps first thing in the morning and I'll be away for the entire ski season. I'm running a nightclub with some mates. Oh, and Rach, I'm dating someone at the moment. I'm actually engaged.'

My heart sinks like a stone. I look back at him, blankly. I can't believe I've misread the situation so completely. I felt certain Alex had been coming on to me. I turn away to hide my obvious disappointment on the pretext of returning my cue to the rack at the far end of the room. It takes me a few moments to gather my composure and by the time I return, I have my mask firmly in place.

'Well, she's a lucky girl,' I finally reply with forced brightness. Inside, I'm angry. Mostly, with myself.

For God's sake, Rach, how on earth did you get that so wrong?

We wave goodbye to each other from across the car park. Another one bites the dust. It will be almost a year before I see him again.

I am minding my own business in a queue at the bank when someone taps me lightly on the shoulder. I turn around and immediately I'm transported back to the night Alex and I met, as I look up into his blue-grey eyes. My heart skips a beat – it begins knocking against the inside of my ribcage. The cashier calls me over. Thinking on my feet, I fire Alex a quick question.

'Are you going to the pub tonight?' I keep my tone light and casual.

'As a matter of fact, I am,' he replies, smiling broadly back at me.

My heart is going so fast I'm beginning to feel a little light-headed. There's the chemistry all over again, only this time, I *know* something is going to happen between us. I'm not sure how I know – I just do.

'Well, I'll see you up there later then.' I flash him a smile before walking over to the cashier with an almost invisible spring in my step.

Alex arrives early at the pub. The moment he spots me, he walks straight over and asks me what I want to drink, before going up to the bar. I'm delighted. Since bumping into him earlier in the day, my mind has been swamped with doubt. *Is Alex now single? Is he interested in me? Am I setting myself up for more disappointment?*

'Last time, I seem to remember it was three-all,' he says, referring to the games of pool we played almost a whole year ago. 'Fancy a decider?' He grins as he hands me my drink. I feel reassured that he's remembered. I hadn't.

'Sure, why not? I take the glass from him and head over to the pool table with a growing sense of déjà vu.

I've often thought about Alex in the last year. He would pop into my head at random times – at work, in the shower, while I was watching TV – but then I would immediately put any thought of him out of my mind by reminding myself he was engaged and now possibly even married.

I watch him set the balls up inside the wooden triangle, and all the while, I'm wondering how to ask him about his fiancée. In the end, I just go for it.

'I thought you might be married by now, Alex.' I shoot him a brief look while pretending to be busy chalking my cue.

Alex lifts the wooden triangle and places it behind him on the window ledge. He doesn't look at me, but replies casually as he stoops to collect the white ball from the opposite end of the pool table.

'It didn't work out,' he says, shrugging his shoulders. He has a gentle way about him, which belies his large frame. I must look relieved, because Alex laughs at me, knowingly.

From that moment on, I know it's only a matter of time before we get together. I already feel as if I've known Alex for a thousand years. I become very aware of him, as we move around the pool table. At times, he stands close enough for me to feel the heat of his body. I can smell his aftershave, and he smells wonderful – clean and fresh.

I notice his muscular arms as he leans over the table to line up his cue. I'm mesmerised by a single prominent vein, which runs like a meandering river down the centre of his bicep. It's the colour of algae. Alex has a fine physique and he seems to be amused by the effect he's having on me. I try to take the focus off my trembling hands by asking him what he's been up to since we last met.

He tells me that he gradually became disillusioned with life in the Alps. His previous ski season was his fourth, and when it was over, he decided to return to England permanently to find himself a job. Now he's working fulltime as a builder and living with friends, only a short distance from the pub. I'm very pleased to hear he won't be leaving again.

'What are *you* up to these days, Rach?' he asks, steering the conversation onto me. I always feel a little uncomfortable discussing my work, but I go ahead and answer.

'I'm still modelling and doing some promotion work. It's ok, I suppose. I've had some interesting jobs, here and there.' I shrug.

Whenever Alex asks me a question, he looks directly into my eyes, without wavering. I find it a little unsettling. He seems to be looking directly into my soul. I soon return my attention to our game of pool.

By closing time, the score is seven-all and *still* no winner, in perhaps the world's longest game of pool. I'm amused by that.

That night, I notice Alex and I are the last two people to leave the pub as we exchange phone numbers outside, in the almost empty car park. I've had one of the best evenings I can remember in a very long time and I'm delighted that we seem to have got off to a flying start, this time around. With careless abandon, I jump in feet first.

CHAPTER 13

It doesn't take much for me to fall hook, line and sinker for Alex. In the meantime, my modelling career takes a nosedive, and so I begin looking around for something different to do with my life. Penny is instrumental in persuading me to find a job as cabin crew. I've grown tired of modelling, but I still have a huge travelling itch to scratch, and the thought of being paid to travel abroad seems enormously appealing.

It isn't long before I've accepted a job with a charter airline and, after four short weeks of training, I find myself working harder than I've ever worked before in my life. The hours are atrocious, and although I love the people I'm working with, we never stay in any of the European destinations. It's very frustrating standing at the bottom of the steps saying goodbye to passengers in either Greece, Turkey or Gran Canaria, only to run back upstairs to the galley kitchen, wolf down a quick meal standing up, and return to the bottom of the steps in time to greet a brand new set of passengers returning home. This is the extent of my travelling – up and down aircraft steps and various strips of airport tarmac dotted around Europe, and then straight back home again. It's not uncommon for me to spend seventeen hours on my feet in one day. I grow tired very, very quickly – physically and mentally – but mostly I'm growing tired of the job. The clincher is being called into the purser's office for a dressing-down because my lipstick isn't visible enough. I've been working to the point of exhaustion for that charter airline, making sure the passengers in my care are well looked after, safe and happy… and all they notice is my bloody lipstick.

Stuff your job. It's time for yet another change.

That evening, I ask Alex to take me to the pub. Penny is already there and I want her advice.

As soon as we arrive, I leave Alex at the bar and I go and look for her. I eventually find her playing pool with a girl I don't recognise.

'Connie, this is Rachel,' Penny says, after greeting me with a huge hug. Connie is leaning over the pool table, lining up a shot. She has dark, cropped hair and elfin features, with a dusting of freckles across her nose. She's wearing an oversized white shirt, denim shorts and a baseball cap, which sits on the very back of her head. Most noticeable, however, are her enormous silver hoop earrings – they're almost touching the green felt on the top of the pool table. She is very pretty in a boyish kind of way.

Connie stops what she's doing and looks at me suspiciously. This makes me laugh, which takes her completely by surprise. She laughs back, almost involuntarily, and her features change instantly. When she smiles, two prominent dimples appear on either side of her face. Suddenly, she looks much younger. I warm to her immediately.

I soon discover that Connie already knows Alex. They greet each other like old friends when he walks into the pool room with our drinks. Connie tells me they went to school together, along with her boyfriend Evan, who is due in the pub at any moment. Penny is standing in the doorway with her arm around Pete, who I've already met. She hasn't known him very long, but already I can see she's smitten. Pete is sandy-haired with green eyes. The chemistry between them is obvious. Alex nods at Pete – they also know each other from their school days.

Five minutes later, Evan walks in and joins the five of us in the pool room. He has bright blue eyes and unusually grey hair for a young man in his early twenties. He's also wearing a baseball cap. He walks up to Connie, leans over, and gives her a kiss on the cheek. His hat falls off.

Right then, I look outside the window and I am sucked into the blackness. The silence. Somewhere across the darkened sky, beyond the stars, the moment is frozen – its roots burrowing deep beneath us in the damp earth.

The six of us are brought together like ivy on a crumbling wall.

This night.

Penny and Pete are the first to get hitched, in a fabulous country-estate wedding. Afterwards, they set up home in a pretty village fifteen miles away, at about the same time as Connie and Evan are splitting up, not for the first time.

Alex, Connie and I begin to spend a lot more time together after that, and before long, the three of us become inseparable. When I'm not working, Connie and I meet up for lunch. We smoke roll-ups and put the world to rights. I'm drawn to her quirky, creative and rather grumpy nature. When she stops frowning, we laugh one hell of a lot.

It isn't long before Alex and I are talking about moving in together. However, this is not without its problems. Alex is lodging at a friend's house, and to my chagrin, I discover that his friend's mother Louise has taken rather a shine to him, and an instant dislike to me. Louise is over twenty years Alex's senior. She wears the face of a woman who rarely smiles, the lines of bitterness deeply etched as a cruel reminder of her unhappy life. She sees Alex as her chance to twist something back from her miserable fate, someone to relieve her loneliness. I see it in her expression as plain as day, as if she were a book to be read. And from the moment Louise learns about me, she tries everything in her power to break us up.

I'm at home watching TV one Saturday evening when I'm visited by two of Alex's friends. They've just come from a surprise birthday party for him, a party I've not been invited to. Louise has arranged it and deliberately left me out. Alex's friends are here to collect me, knowing that he wants me there, but I'm not prepared to walk into the lion's den.

'I'm really sorry. I just wouldn't feel right going without an invite,' I explain, with a mixture of anger and indignation. It's sweet they've come to get me, but I don't feel like squaring up to Louise in front of all of his friends. It would be embarrassing for everyone. I sit back down on the sofa and turn the TV off. My anger is much too loud for me to concentrate on anything else.

The next morning, Alex comes over, a little worse for wear.

'Good party was it, last night?' I say, tight-lipped. I haven't slept much at all. As far as I'm concerned, Louise has thrown down the gauntlet, but I want to know how Alex feels about my non-invite.

'Well, it was thoughtful of Louise to throw a party for me, Rach. But she should've invited you too. I really wanted you there,' he says, a little sheepishly.

'She bloody well hates me, Alex!' I shout back. The anger, which I've been trying to suppress, erupts like a torrent of water, bursting through a dam. 'She's hardly going to invite me to a surprise party for you. She fancies you, and you know it. It's *really* creepy!' I'm yelling, but I can see he isn't in the mood for an angry barrage. Louise has put Alex up for several months now for free, and I realise this isn't the best way to get him on my side. I take a deep breath and try my best to calm down. 'Alex, do you want a cup of tea?' I concede, changing the subject.

This is the very first hurdle I have to cross in our relationship. There are many more to come.

Within a few months, Alex and I find a two-bedroomed, mid-terraced house to buy right opposite the house that I've been renting. It needs a lot of work, but Alex is confident he can do most of the renovation, with my help.

We set to work as soon as we have the keys. We strip years of paint and plaster from the walls; we pull up floors and rip out the old bathroom and kitchen; we fill several skips to overflowing with the clutter and cladding of many others who once lived in that house, until the dust is lying thick in our hair. And then we get to work, making it our own. With the radio blaring, we sand, plaster, paint, tile and varnish every surface from top to bottom, until our backs ache and our hands are calloused and raw. Every single night, we fall into bed exhausted. In less than six months, every inch of that house has either been renovated, renewed or replaced. It's been a labour of love, but together, Alex and I have created the perfect home for ourselves and I'm as proud as punch. For the first time in as long as I can remember, I have hope for a happy future.

One day, I come home from work to find Louise sitting in her car outside our house. Her face is obscured by the light on her windscreen, but I can see she's been crying. I ignore her. I walk past, put my key in the door and walk in. *Now she is stalking me.* When I tell Alex, he is silent.

I visit Louise a few days later. I show up on *her* doorstep. She invites me in for a cup of tea. I watch her in her lonely kitchen, gnarled fingers like branches curled around her mug. I see her pain. Sunken eyes. Raw. Like the stewing steak by the side of her enamel sink. It drips. Her pain is not for me or Alex. It is hers to keep and I am mindful of it. I do not finish my tea. I leave. She will not bother us again. And she doesn't.

I soon discover that Connie and Alex have something in common. They both like to smoke cannabis. I've only experimented with it before now, but I'm curious. I ask Connie if I can try some when I'm over at her house one evening. She is already stoned.

I watch her stick two Rizla cigarette papers together with the gum of a third. Then, using her lighter, she burns the very corner of a dark brown cube of Moroccan hashish and breaks a tiny piece off, crumbling it evenly throughout the papers. I can smell the distinctive aroma as it drifts under my nose. She sprinkles a generous amount of tobacco on top of the crumbled cannabis, and she picks up the entire joint. Using her fingers and thumbs, she licks the gum on the nearside edge of the papers, flips the open edge closed with her two index fingers and skilfully seals it. I look down at the perfectly rolled joint. She taps one end on the kitchen table, smiles and hands it over.

I light it, inhale deeply, and hold my breath for a few seconds. Slowly, I exhale, watching the smoke as it curls upwards. Without warning, I cough, expelling the rest of the smoke in my lungs. I splutter, struggling to catch my breath. My eyes are watering and Connie is now laughing at me.

'You inhaled a bit too much, Rach.' She smiles at me with puffy, bloodshot eyes. 'Try again, but this time don't have so much.'

I inhale again. This time, I manage to hold the smoke in my lungs without coughing. I pass the joint to Connie and sit back in my chair to assess what I am feeling.

The very top of my head is now tight, as if I've put on a hat that is much too small. The ringing in my ears becomes pronounced, and I begin to feel as if I'm floating. My mind is now detached from my body and is slowly growing away from me, encompassing everything it touches along the way – separate from me and yet connected at the same time. I feel as if I'm falling *into* myself while my mind is expanding *out* from my body. Nothing really matters. I become the Observer and I like this perspective. Everything looks different, somehow. Familiar items seem alien, but in an interesting way. It's as if I'm seeing objects for the very first time. I'm staring at the lighter in my hand now, and Connie laughs. I immediately crash back into the kitchen. I can feel the chair against my back and the seat cushion under my buttocks.

'You ok?' she asks, amused.

'Yeah. I feel kinda weird. I can't really explain it. Like I'm drunk.' I begin to laugh. Suddenly, everything seemed ridiculously funny and I can't stop. Connie joins in. I like this feeling.

Connie's mother arrives home and pokes her head around the door. Suddenly, I feel very self-conscious, although I do my very best to appear normal.

'Hi,' I attempt to smile at her, but I'm finding it impossible to control my face. I'm fighting hard to maintain my composure and not at all sure If I'm leering at her. Connie's mother looks at us both with an expression I can't quite fathom, but it makes me feel anxious and a little paranoid. Now *this* is an entirely new feeling.

I don't like this feeling.

However, over the coming days, it doesn't stop me asking Connie and Alex for a drag on their joints. I love the initial feeling I experience when I get high. Very quickly, I become addicted to it.

I haven't been smoking for very long, a few weeks at most, when I am aware that something else is creeping around inside my head; some kind of tar-black monster is sewing tiny little seeds of fear and doubt into the furthest corners of my mind. Its movements are almost imperceptible.

Shadows.

I hear a voice.

A whisper.

It isn't a voice that speaks with words. Grey-black mist. Twisting forms. Teeth. *Rot.* This is how it feels.

Like someone is standing over me.

I shiver. *I am Cold.*

The voice is almost inaudible – an eerie whisper.

But it grows.

Loud.

My fear is growing with it. Writhing inside it. Trapped.

Until I am afraid of everything.

Me.

The three of us are in my sitting room smoking a joint. We have just got back from the pub. We are stoned. Laughing. But I begin to feel uncomfortable. Alex is looking at Connie intently. He is looking at her as if there is something he isn't saying. A shared secret. Unseen. All of a sudden, it seems obvious to me, the Observer. The way she looks back at him confirms my suspicions. She nods and looks directly into his eyes. Those eyes that I love.

Silently, I continue to watch them interacting with each other while we talk about things. Ridiculous things. I have no interest in our conversation. I am telling myself the exchange I witnessed between them was perfectly innocent. But the tar-black monster is whispering to me. It's convincing me otherwise. While we're talking about ridiculous things.

That night, another dark seed is planted. *Alex is having an affair with Connie.*

As time passes, my nagging doubts begin to affect my friendship with Connie. Paranoia makes me question her loyalty towards me. I feel trapped and don't know what's real anymore. It's a horrible feeling. I'm addicted to the out-of-body high, whenever I smoke cannabis, but I'm increasingly unable to separate it from my fear.

As if things aren't bad enough, my paranoia is no longer confined to the times when I'm stoned, but it now begins to raise its ugly head when I'm quite lucid — at work or at any other time of the day or night. I become very frightened.

As my fear continues to grow, Connie's on-off relationship with Evan is suddenly back on again. The relief I feel is palpable. Alex and I see much less of her and I am grateful for that.

Connie and Evan become the second couple in our group to get hitched. After the wedding, they move up to London. I continue to smoke heavily with Alex every single night. I begin to feel isolated and increasingly paranoid.

My radio alarm goes off, rousing me from a deep sleep, from that peaceful place of nothingness. Alex has already left for work and I am alone. Almost immediately, I feel fear creeping up from somewhere beneath the bed. It envelops me like a dark grey mist, cold and damp. I groan and pull the duvet tight around me. I am shivering. I want to wrap myself up tighter and go back to sleep, go back to that place where I'm not aware of anything at all. Where I'm not scared anymore.

My heart is beating fast. I feel hot. Nauseous. *Clammy.* This is a relatively new feeling. The noise of the radio taunts me, mercilessly.

Get up, Rachel. Get going.

Impossible.

I can't face work. Not today. I feel utterly miserable.

This is the first day I call in sick.

It's the first of many.

The months pass, and I retreat further and further inside my head, into a self-inflicted kind of depression. I manage to emerge long enough to hold down my job. *Just.*

Very soon, this feeling becomes familiar. My normal. Everyone is dull and grey. Like me.

Despite this, I slowly move through the ranks at work as others grow bored and leave. I feel safe. No one sees me.

I am the walls.

In a little less than four years, I am promoted to manager. I'm a manager of grey walls. At work, I talk about things that are safe — work-related things. No one has the remotest idea of the torment going on inside my head every single day. Only the tar-black monster knows — my only true friend throughout those lonely years. When I leave work, the fight returns. The fight to know what's real. It is utterly exhausting. I am going through the motions.

I am lonely.

The more isolated I feel, the more I crave something solid. Work isn't enough, nor is home. I want children. I want a family. I think back to my relationship with Ben, the only other man I'd wanted to marry. With each passing day, I become increasingly insecure. What I really want is a commitment from Alex.

'Why don't we get married, Alex?' I suggest lightly. Today, I feel especially good. It's Saturday morning, the sun is shining warm and bright outside our bedroom window, and Alex and I are entwined in each other. We've just made love.

'Cup of tea?' Alex replies, untangling himself and getting out of bed.

I watch his naked bottom retreating out of the room. *Another time, Rach.* I roll over onto my back and slide up to a sitting position.

Each time I mention marriage, Alex changes the subject. I know he loves me, but I'm becoming more and more frustrated with his refusal to commit. It feels like being with Ben all over again.

And then everything changes. I'm not sure why.

Alex and I decide to go away on holiday with Penny, Pete, Evan and Connie, to Barbados. Mainly because I want Alex to meet my parents. Together, the six of us rent a house on the beach, but all too soon, I begin to struggle terribly with my demons.

Almost immediately, Alex scores a small amount of cannabis and Connie and I are sharing a joint with him on the beach. Just like the old days, only in nicer surroundings.

Later, we all come up from the beach to make ourselves a drink and watch the sunset. I've seen it a thousand times already. This time, I'm scared.

I sit out on the terrace with a rum and 7 Up in my hand. The ice tinkles against the glass when I sip it. One by one, the others join me to watch the sun, now low on the horizon – a huge fiery ball against the velvet-blue sky. Calypso music is playing on the radio, drifting in from the house behind us, providing a rhythmic lull to accompany the scene unfolding before our eyes. The sky changes in colour and intensity. With each passing moment, it is different – from orange to crimson with flashes of gold and purple. The scent of rum and suntan lotion rises on a gentle breeze. The sun dips further as the waves break against the coral-pink and white sands, less than two hundred metres in front of us.

I am in paradise. *I should be happy.* But inside, I'm miserable.

The others laugh and chatter together on either side of me. Like morning birds, it's a happy sound. But all I want is to return to the sanctuary and safety of my house back in England — to the grey mizzle. I no longer know myself. This Rachel who watches the sunset.

I am terrified of *me.*

The holiday progresses, and the voice inside my head convinces me *again* that something is going on between Alex and Connie. I become hyper-vigilant, listening intently to everything they say to each other. Over breakfast. On the beach. *Everywhere.* It becomes a living-hell-on-earth inside my head. But there is nowhere for me to run.

I do my very best to remain calm on the outside, but all the while, I feel as if I'm tearing out my hair and screaming at the top of my lungs – *in total silence.* Madness is doing its damnedest to claim me.

If only I had the strength to tell everyone – anyone – what I was going through. If only I had the strength to stop smoking cannabis.

Alex and Connie continue to smoke around me, completely oblivious to my torment. I don a mask of calm and I carry on. Smoking, mostly. *Ridiculous, stupid me.*

During that time-of-no-escape, I see my mother only once. Strangely, it's one of the very few times I actually feel sane. Perhaps her madness has a sobering effect on me.

She's accompanied by my half-brother Mike, and that night she's in great spirits and clearly happy to see me again. To be honest, I'm grateful for the distraction. Mum is very different with me now, almost unrecognisable from the monster of my childhood. Most significantly, that evening, I discover a completely new way of relating to her.

I watch her chatting away to Alex and my friends with the ease and experience of someone accustomed to entertaining many a guest over the years. I know this superficial side to her well enough, but before now, I would cringe inwardly observing it. This time, however, I imagine her to be some kind of eccentric aunt. I don't think about her as my mother anymore, nor the embarrassment of it. I'm surprised at how well this seems to work. Almost immediately, I experience a greater degree of emotional distance from her, which gives me permission to write off her rather off-beat, grandiose behaviour.

Great Aunt Carmen.

It has a certain ring to it.

On the last day of our holiday, I finally find a reprieve. We decide to drive over to the east coast in two small cars we've hired. Our first stop is the Crane Beach.

We all pile out of the cars and make our way to the top of the cliff to take in one of the best views on the island. Alex holds back to talk to a Rasta with a gold-toothed grin and a huge multi-coloured knitted cap on the top of his head, filled with dreadlocks. He's selling jewellery out of a briefcase, but I assume Alex is trying to score some more weed.

'We'll carry on down and find a spot on the beach,' I say to Alex, a little frustrated. The rest of us walk down the steep path, picking our way along the narrow uneven track. The path snakes around the edge of the cliff and, halfway down, the rock juts out sharply, creating a natural overhang and a sheer drop down to the sea below. There, we encounter two young men in surf shorts, with deep tans, preparing to jump into the water. They time their jump between the crashing of the waves and we stop to watch for a few moments. I feel their adrenaline. One after the other, they jump. The waves swallow them up and we continue to watch as they reappear on the surface and swim away from the cliff, into deeper water, bobbing in the swell, which obscures them from view as they dip under the waves. Their progress back to the beach is slow, but they are now a safe distance from the rocks. I exhale – I hadn't realised I was holding my breath. Several others pass us on their way up, dripping wet, with thick sand stuck to their feet. Their excitement – like a charge of electricity as they stride up the path – passes through me.

Eventually, the footpath leads us down to the bottom of the cliff, onto perfect white sand. I kick off my flip-flops and sink my feet into the soft warmth of the beach. I curl my toes into it. I want to be inside it. At the far end, golden palms rise up proudly, their tops bowing gently in the Atlantic breeze, like elderly giants before a dance. In this fleeting moment, the darkness lifts.

We find a space about halfway down the beach, and I'm beginning to spread my towel out on a sun lounger when I see Alex approaching. I sit on the lounger, on the edge of it, and reach into my bag for a bottle of suntan lotion.

High above us, perched at the very top of the cliff, six white pillars rise up behind a balustrade of pink coral stone around the hotel's swimming pool. Suddenly, a memory captures me – I'm a child swimming underwater with a mask, a blue one. The water is cold and I can see a large crab on the bottom of the pool. I swim down and poke it with my finger. White and yellow angry pincers. *It's alive!* At the bottom of the pool. On top of the cliff.

I smile to myself at that.

A lone blackbird crosses a clear blue sky; lighter at the edges, a deeper blue above. I watch it arc around and disappear behind the rock. The sand, scratching between my toes when I wriggle them in deeper. Tiny grains. The warmth under my feet. Encased. The vast expanse of space all around me. This moment in time. This photograph never taken. This picture in my mind.

Alex casts a shadow across me. He's standing in front of me, the sun a dazzling white behind his silhouette. I shield my eyes to see him as he sinks down. There's a flash of sunlight, bold and bright. He is kneeling in front of me. I'm puzzled. He is grinning at me, watery-eyed.

'Rachel. Will you marry me?' he asks softly.

He's holding out a polished charcoal-grey hematite ring. It stands upright, his fingers and thumb around it, shiny like mercury. Poised. So, *this* is what he bought from the Rasta. I'm stunned. Trembling. I look around in disbelief. Penny, Pete, Connie and Evan are grinning back at us. *Frozen.* My vision blurs.

Alex wants to marry me!

I want to jump up and skip along the beach. I want to scream at the top of my voice. Instead, I hold out my ring finger for him. My hand is shaking. A tear falls into my lap.

'Alex… *Of course* I'll marry you!'

Joy floods into me from the blue, blue sky above. It reaches through me. Inside of me. I can't catch my breath.

Every single one of my doubts – the cloying fear I've been so desperate to hide – is *gone*. Like mist. Alex slides the ring onto my finger. It fits perfectly. On this perfect day.

Finally, the tar-black monster is silent.

CHAPTER 14

Eighteen months after Alex proposed to me on the Crane Beach, a group of over fifty of us, including Penny, Pete, Evan and Connie, travel back to Barbados for the wedding.

We commandeer three villas next to one another on the beach. Alex's stepfather Robert, his wife Beth, Alex's sister and her boyfriend, along with Alex's stepsister, have chosen to stay in exactly the same villa we were renting the previous year. A few hundred yards away, under the canopy of rustling Casuarina trees, in a pretty pink coral stone villa, is my sister Philippa, and her family. Me, Alex, Connie and Evan, and four of Alex's close friends, move into the third and largest villa. There are also several other guests staying in various hotels and guest houses nearby. They will join us on the wedding day at the end of the week.

Keeping with tradition, I make the decision to stay with Penny and Pete the night before the wedding. Tucked away under a shock of fuchsia bougainvillea, in the next bay, I wake up early in the spare bedroom of their rented villa.

I have butterflies in my stomach. *Whoosh!*

So many times, I've dreamt about this day, and here it is. I stretch and turn onto my side to look out of the window. There isn't a cloud in the sky as I listen to the morning chorus of blackbirds welcoming the day. *Our wedding day!*

Penny pokes her head around the door and smiles at me. 'Tea?' She yawns, rubbing her eyes.

'Is it too early for a rum?' I laugh, nervously. 'I can't believe I'm actually getting married today, Penny.' I sit up and swing my legs down to the tiled floor. My dress and veil are hanging at the far end of the room in a white suit bag. I unzip the bag, carefully remove my dress and hang it back over the wardrobe door. I stand back to look at it for the millionth time. It's off-white and slim-fitting, with sheer sleeves and a very small train at the back. Simple and elegant. I notice that the train is a little crumpled, but the creases will soon fall out. The veil is also creased. I had to fold it over a few times to make it fit inside the bag. I take it out and hang it up next to my dress. Walking backwards, I carefully spread out the folds of tulle, running my fingers along the cream satin piping. My heart turns over again. *Oh, God.* I feel a little sick. *I'm actually getting married!*

Penny is a trouper. My nerves are threatening to get the better of me and eventually she presents me with the rum I jokingly mentioned earlier. The ice tinkles like a glass chandelier in a gentle breeze as I take a sip. The condensation on the outside of the glass is cool against my nervous palm. I quickly feel the rum reach the very ends of my toes and almost instantly, I am calmer.

'Thanks Penny.' I sigh, raising my glass to her. She laughs at my obvious relief.

Connie and Philippa join us a little later that morning. I've asked the three of them to be my bridesmaids and to wear anything cheerful and suitable for a Caribbean wedding. Penny is wearing a layered blue chiffon mini-dress, Connie, a sheer pastel green trouser suit and Philippa, a golden-bronze satin shift. They look like fondant fancies on a fine china plate. It's thirty degrees outside and I'm grateful for the air conditioning in Penny's villa as I'm beginning to sweat.

Before Pete leaves, he tells us what happened during an impromptu stag night the previous evening. I already know about it – Alex admitted it to me just as I was leaving for Penny's villa, laden with all my wedding paraphernalia. I wasn't very happy, but I said nothing. We're scheduled to be married at four in the afternoon and I really want Alex to be fresh and rested. *More fool me.*

Apparently, Pete is saying, Alex made it back to our villa at five o'clock that morning, falling over drunk. *Why is he telling me this? What state will Alex be in today?* For the first time that holiday, my heart sinks.

'The taxi is here!' Connie shouts.

'*Shit!*' I can't stop thinking about Alex. *Will he be ok?*

I'm sitting in the back of the taxi. Penny, Connie and Philippa are chattering excitedly around me, when the tar-black monster begins to whisper in my ear.

'*Not now!*' I scream inside my head. I am beginning to feel desperate, terrified I might fall into the dark mist, which is creeping around the edges of my mind like a spidery shadow. Stalking me. I watch the sun through the car window as it flashes between the trees against a cloudless blue sky. I close my eyes. It flashes through my eyelids.

Go.

Away.

Right then, the taxi pulls up into the car park of the marina hotel where we'll be catching a speedboat for the next part of our journey.

'Rachel?' Penny's voice brings me crashing back to reality. She's already out of the car, reaching in to grab my hand. Suddenly I remember, and my heart lurches.

I'm getting married!

I feel her fingers closing around mine. She pulls me out – out of the shadows. Penny has no idea that her grip does so much more than help me to my feet. All of a sudden, it's bright again, inside my head.

We're escorted to a sleek white-and-yellow speedboat, moored up directly opposite the hotel's marina bar. This allows just enough time for a swift rum punch before we're asked to remove our sandals and climb aboard. The boat rocks precariously as we settle, a little awkwardly, into the cream leather seats at the rear of the boat. My heart begins to hammer away inside my chest. *Well, this is it, Rach.*

Twenty minutes later, I finally spot the bright yellow twin hulls of the catamaran where Alex and I have chosen to be married. The yacht is anchored in the seclusion of the very same bay where I had woken up that morning, in Penny and Pete's villa.

I stand up, excited. My veil catches the wind and it fans out behind me like a sail. The speedboat's engine slows and Penny, Connie and Philippa jump to their feet, calling out to the sea of smiling faces as we slowly circle the yacht. I'm close enough to see my mother, father, and my three brothers standing together, grinning and waving back at me. Doing my very best to stay upright, I wave back – a wobbly moment of pure joy.

Penny grabs my veil and holds it above her head to stop it from trailing in the water as we moor up alongside the yacht. I can hear my father's voice as I'm helped aboard by one of the yacht's crew in my bare feet. Penny carefully places the shorter part of the veil over my face, and she gently squeezes both my shoulders. Before I have time to think, she spins me around. Dad is right there in front of me.

'You're a knockout, Rachel.' He beams proudly, taking my arm for the few feet it will take for me to walk up to Alex in my bare feet. We haven't rehearsed this, Dad and I. It just happens. I look up through the haze of my veil and finally, I see him standing a little way ahead of me. Alex is grinning from ear to ear. His face is shiny with sweat. My heart is beating fast.

As I approach him, I notice two dark patches under each arm of his lime green shirt. With one final step, I am standing next to him, our shoulders now touching. I can feel the heat of his arm through the sheer sleeve of my dress. My mouth is as dry as the sand on the beach, directly in my eyeline fifty-or-so yards away.

Alex looks down at me briefly. He's sallow-faced. Dusky shadows are smudged beneath his eyes. He looks a little green around the gills but I don't care one bit about that. I'm just relieved that he's made it. Somewhere deep inside the recesses of my mind, a profound and unrelenting fear that Alex might not show up today, a fear I've been doing my utmost to ignore all morning, blows away on the balmy breeze. *Poof.* My heart begins to soar. Suddenly, I'm aware of all our guests standing in a semicircle around us. I feel them.

This is really happening.

We are married by a female bishop. She steps forward wearing a floor-length purple gown. Hers are the leather lace-up boots, cast to one side with all the shoes and sparkly sandals. We are all barefoot on deck; the wood is warm and smooth underfoot. In straight lines. *My mother will like this,* I'm thinking.

In a golden sky, with our shadows growing longer as the sun dips low on the horizon, Alex and I become husband and wife.

With newly-ringed fingers wrapped around each others',
we carefully cut into our nautical-themed wedding cake. Alex
trembles slightly beneath my fingers. *Is he nervous?* I can't be
certain. Right then, Mum taps me gently on the shoulder.
I turn around and, without hesitation, I give her a big bear
hug. Alex does too. She looks sensational in her flowing gold
and deep blue caftan. Like a rare exotic bird. She is smiling
broadly, perfectly at ease in this environment. It feels right for
her to be here with me.

When it's time for everyone to disembark, Alex and I
sneak off to the next bay. By now it is dark. I waste no time in
stripping off and I run, headlong and naked, into the sea. A
loud splash and a shriek as I hit the water – the only sound in
the inky-black darkness. I call out to Alex, who quickly follows,
laughing at my enthusiasm. We don't wait to get back to the
villa. I wrap my naked legs around him and we consummate
our marriage right there in the cool, Caribbean Sea, below a
million shining stars.

Nothing can take you away from me now.

The next morning, Alex and I set off on our honeymoon,
taking a short flight via Antigua to Tortola, in the British
Virgin Islands. We are taken to the dock in Tortola where we
climb aboard a high-speed water taxi to the island of Virgin
Gorda. I can't hear what Alex is saying to me above the
noise of the engine. We both laugh and give up talking until
we arrive in the small harbour. My hair is all over the place.
I'm excited.

My father has booked us into a private villa in Little Dix
Bay. It's his wedding present to us. Our villa is set in lush
tropical gardens on a gently sloping hill. The building is clad
in yellow slatted wood and it has white louvred shutters over

the windows. We walk up the wooden stairs and step inside. At the far end of the villa, facing the sea, a large bamboo curtain is rolled up to reveal several blue-green islands across the bay. They rise up from the crystal-clear, turquoise water – pure white sands surrounding each one – separating the land from the sea.

I put my bag down to take it all in. The furniture inside the villa is natural and sparse. The linen, crisp and expensive. Egyptian cotton. I run the flat of my hand over the cool sheets. There are candles in glass jars on either side of the thick-set mahogany bed, not yet lit. A promise of the night. The scent is cedar and ylang-ylang. Exotic. The silence slips around us. An enticement.

Now, this really is paradise.

On our very first morning, we hire a small motorboat and go exploring, stopping briefly a few feet away from the shores of Necker Island, with its famous entrepreneur owner.

We swim naked with sea turtles in the aquamarine waters around Honeymoon Island. Like Robinson Crusoe, we sit on the rocks and watch a pelican catching his supper – a huge grey fish – which thrashes from side to side inside the pelican's accordion-like beak. A fine spray fans out from its fins and its tail, like a net. Eventually, the fish disappears down the pelican's impossibly narrow neck.

Spreading wide its wings, the pelican flaps repeatedly and then it's airborne, heavy at first, like an amphibious aircraft. It flies, seemingly in slow motion, becoming an enormous expanse of wing in silhouette against a purple sky.

Never before have I known such a delicious sense of freedom. After five long days in paradise with Alex, I want the feeling to go on forever.

CHAPTER 15

Much too soon, Alex and I are retracing our steps to Barbados for one last night, before returning home to England. The holiday, the wedding and our honeymoon have managed to keep my spirits buoyed for quite some time.

Naïvely, I start to believe that my fears have gone for good, but little by little I begin to feel paranoid all over again. It's very small, almost imperceptible things at first. I find myself scrutinising Alex's behaviour, particularly if we're in the company of other women. He is very charming towards women in particular. The ridiculous idea that he's looking for something more from any other female he talks to takes root inside my fractured mind, and without me being fully aware of it, I've opened the door, once again, to the tar-black monster.

A few weeks after our wedding, I discover I'm pregnant. I am overjoyed. I'm also very surprised to find that my feelings of fear have disappeared. All of a sudden, it occurs to me that whenever I'm feeling genuinely happy, the tar-black monster just isn't there anymore. It comes rushing back in whenever I'm afraid – when I allow myself to be led by my fears.

I can control it.

I think.

This time, I make absolutely certain that everything is going to be right for the life growing inside of me. *This* time, I'm married, I have a home... and a job that provides me with maternity leave. At thirty-two, I really can't wait to be a mother and I'm very excited about telling Alex.

I have to wait all day. I'm bursting with excitement. The moment Alex walks through the door from work, I hand him a glass of champagne.

'Alex, I'm pregnant.' I beam up at him. He looks back at me, confused. My smile drops. This isn't quite what I was expecting. 'You're going to be a father!' I smile again, hopefully. Alex doesn't smile back, nor does he take the glass from me. He just looks at me with a blank expression on his face. My heart sinks. He walks into the sitting room and sits down heavily on one of our cream fabric sofas. I put his glass down on the coffee table in front of him. He looks terrified. I sit down next to him, put my glass down and gently pick up one of his rough, calloused hands. I'm transported back to a conversation we had very early on in our relationship.

We are sitting on a hill under a huge oak tree in the local deer park and Alex is telling me about his family.

'I was six when my dad died and fifteen when my mum died,' he says flatly. He's hunched over, picking at the grass, uneasy in his thoughts. I am shocked. 'Mum married Robert a couple of years after dad died. Much too soon for me. Robert used to work with my dad. I couldn't stand him.'

By this time, I've already met Alex's step-parents, Robert and Beth. I immediately noticed the tension between Alex and his stepfather. Alex tells me that the only reason he hasn't completely cut his stepfather out of his life is because of Beth. Robert married her a few years after losing Alex's mother. Beth is a no-nonsense, down-to-earth woman who speaks her mind and recognises the importance of family. She has two grown-up children of her own but they live some distance away. Despite that, she manages to keep the entire family together with the strength of her unwavering love. I warm to her instantly. Alex and I are never left out of Christmas gatherings, or any other special family occasions. Robert, on the other hand, is very quiet and reserved. That doesn't bother me. It's just him.

Alex also tells me about his sister, Dorothy, or Dot, as he calls her. He adores her, and when we eventually meet, I can see why. She is excited and enthusiastic about life and she only ever sees the good in everyone. Dot is the only immediate family Alex has left in the world, and their bond is obvious.

I pick up my champagne glass from the coffee table and take a sip. The bubbles fizz on my tongue.

'Alex, I know you're scared, but you really don't need to be. It's going to be fine.' I squeeze his hand and smile again. This time, I see a glimmer of something in his eyes. Hope, perhaps, but I'm not too sure.

Despite Alex's fears, I launch myself wholeheartedly into becoming a mother. I simply can't contain my enthusiasm. The very next day, I'm already buying a few things for the baby: two baby grows, four pairs of tiny white socks and a white cotton hat. I even find a wallpaper border – something to turn our spare room into a nursery. It has baby rabbits on it, chasing each other.

At six weeks' pregnant, I have a miscarriage. I'm utterly devastated.

I take a week off work and mope around the house in my dressing gown, mostly hiding under the duvet cover. Alex does his very best to cheer me up, but I resent his concern. Somehow, it doesn't feel authentic to me.

'You ok?' He sits down on the bed and puts a steaming hot cup of tea on the bedside table next to me. I don't answer. I just want to cry.

'No.' I don't want to talk. I turn away.

I feel the weight of Alex's hand on top of the duvet. It's resting lightly on my hip, but I don't find his touch reassuring. I shake it off. *Just go away.*

It's not his fault. *At least, I hope it's not.*

Paranoia has set in all over again. It takes everything I have to drag myself back to work. I don't say what's happened. I tell them all I had the flu.

Life is dull and grey for several months after that. Winter comes and goes and I'm afraid and unhappy for most of that time. At work, I wear an everything-is-ok mask and get on with the job, but really, I'm struggling under the surface, spiralling down into a very dark place.

I feel much too ashamed to share what I'm feeling with anyone, not even Alex. I can't tell him because he's the reason behind so much of my fear. I just don't feel I can trust him anymore, but I'm not entirely sure why that is. There's absolutely no evidence of him being unfaithful to me, but I just can't shake off my paranoia. I'm not thinking rationally, but I don't really know what rational is anymore. This frightens me the most.

Somewhere in my consciousness, I have a vague realisation that cannabis is having a detrimental effect on me. Alex continues to smoke cannabis every single night. He never forces me to smoke with him, but I feel completely powerless to stop.

This is addiction at its worst. I am an addict.

How the hell did this happen?

Initially, it seemed so harmless, smoking a joint with Alex and Connie – like having a drink after work, Alex once said, laughing. Only Alex doesn't drink much at all, because he suffers with migraines and alcohol often triggers them.

I soon learn exactly *why* Alex smokes cannabis every day. To an outsider, it must seem obvious, but it takes a while for me to make the connection.

I've known from the very beginning of our relationship that Alex started to smoke cannabis almost immediately after his mother's death, when he was only fifteen years old. He said that it was the only thing that helped him to forget. He didn't have any counselling after his mother died and, therefore, he found another way to numb his pain; to escape his *own* tar-black monster, I suppose. Ultimately, he learned to lessen the pain of losing both of his parents at such a young age, by self-medicating with cannabis. And, every single night, for thirteen years, Alex has been trying to forget. In many ways, who can blame him?

I need to sort myself out, and quick. My problems aren't Alex's fault.

I let him off the hook.

Only a few months after my miscarriage, I'm pregnant again. I'm ecstatic and *this* time, Alex seems pleased with the news.

However, my delight is short-lived because at exactly six weeks, I miscarry again. I feel numb and confused for days. I go and see the doctor, who suggests that Alex and I have some routine blood tests, but they all come back inconclusive.

Almost unbelievably, for the third time in less than eight months, I am pregnant again. I'm absolutely petrified. I won't allow myself to get excited as I approach the fateful six-week-point when my body previously rejected the tiny life growing inside of me. Twice. This time, I keep my pregnancy all to myself. I don't even tell Alex, not at first.

Six weeks come and go and this time, my little baby stays put. Every morning, I cry with relief behind locked doors, but still I keep my pregnancy all to myself.

At eight weeks pregnant, I decide to pay for a private scan. I really need some reassurance that everything is going to be ok this time. I only tell Alex over the phone, literally just before the scan, and I go along to the private hospital on my own. He's at work and I ask him to meet me at the hospital in time for the appointment.

I sit on my own in the squeaky-clean waiting room, checking the time on an oversized clock on the wall every two minutes, with my heart in my mouth.

What if there's no heartbeat?

What if there's no baby?

I've convinced myself that something is wrong by the time a door opens at the far end of the waiting room and a woman calls out my name.

'Rachel Langley?' Her voice echoes across the empty waiting room.

'Yes!' I stand up much too quickly and instantly feel light-headed. I look back to the entrance doors, but Alex still hasn't arrived. I'll have to carry on without him. There's a lump forming in my throat as I fight back my tears.

Pull yourself together, Rach.

My heart is threatening to jump out of my chest and my legs are wobbly. I'm grateful to lie back on the bed, which creaks noisily under me in the small consulting room.

The doctor is very pleasant and kind. She asks me all kinds of questions, which I struggle to answer; I am fixated on the screen at the far end of the bed.

I think the doctor recognises my eagerness to discover what's going on inside of me, because she stops talking, smiles and applies freezing cold gel to my exposed lower abdomen. She places the scanner in the clear gel and begins to move it around. The black and white shapes on the screen are blurred and indistinguishable. I can't see anything that looks like a baby. The doctor keeps moving the scanner around my belly, pressing down in places, trying to find something recognisable.

Still nothing.

I am now beginning to panic.

And then I see it!

A pulsating shape of new life. My baby's rapidly beating heart.

'There it is,' she says with a grin. I burst into tears. Hot tears of utter relief slide down the side of my face as I lay back on the bed, looking at my unborn child. *My baby is alive.*

'There's another one!' the doctor cries suddenly. On the screen in front of me, I can clearly see two rapidly beating hearts. 'You have twins!' she says, as she turns to look at me.

Just then, there's a loud knock on the door. It's Alex. I've completely forgotten he's due to meet me. The doctor gets up and lets him in. He sits down on a chair next to the bed and slowly takes in the news, looking anxiously between me and the doctor. He cries, too. He's as happy as I am.

We both leave the consulting room on a cloud. This pregnancy feels very different. Somehow, I just know that things are going to be ok as we hold hands and walk out across the car park.

The very next day, I arrive at the airport early, with Penny and Connie, to catch a morning flight to Jordan. Weeks earlier, the three of us arranged to go away together for five days, to a spa hotel on the Dead Sea.

I decide not to tell them that I'm pregnant. I want to wait for the obligatory three months to pass before I tell anyone. Our break is perfectly timed and neither Penny nor Connie seems to notice that I'm no longer drinking alcohol or smoking. I suppose it's the ideal opportunity for a detox and they never once question me.

In the warmth of the Jordanian sunshine, as I'm cooling myself off in the infinity pool, I realise that I'm no longer feeling scared. My paranoia has completely disappeared.

It's always so much worse when I'm all alone with my thoughts. Whenever I'm with Penny and Connie, we chat away incessantly and there isn't much time to allow the tar-black monster in. Crucially, I stopped smoking cannabis weeks ago, as soon as I discovered I was pregnant – *that*, more than anything else, made the difference to how I feel.

My wonderful secret, the beautiful surroundings and all of the relaxing treatments have a deliciously cathartic effect on me. In stark contrast to the thick grey mud, which is covering me from head to toe, my mind is crystal clear.

I breathe a huge sigh of relief.

At exactly three months' pregnant, I finally announce that Alex and I are expecting twins. Everyone is genuinely delighted for us.

Not long after our announcement, Penny tells me that she's also pregnant. At first, I'm surprised, but I'm genuinely pleased for her. I hadn't even realised that Penny and Pete were trying for a baby. I don't think I would have been quite so happy if she'd announced her pregnancy while I was still wallowing in the misery of my two miscarriages. I would have been envious.

As it turns out, Penny and I form a bond that happens naturally when two women are pregnant together.

For a time, life feels very good again.

CHAPTER 16

Almost seven months later, exactly eight days before
Christmas, I go into labour. Alex and I are both terrified.
Will I be able to cope? Will my babies be ok?

Alex is frightened because the day has finally
arrived – *fatherhood*.

We drive to the hospital with my enormous belly
contracting into a kind of torpedo – my strange, alien body,
full of babies.

I am under the bright white lights of the operating room,
surrounded by an alarming amount of hospital staff hidden
behind blue paper masks and starched green gowns. I'm
having a caesarean.

Finn, who is breach, is pulled from my belly at exactly
12.07 p.m. They cut his umbilical cord, wipe him down and
swaddle him with a skill that comes from a conveyor belt of
deliveries. They hand him to Alex. By now, Finn is screaming
at the top of his lungs as I lie helpless and flat on my back,
unable to move anything except for my torso.

With the widest of smiles, I watch Alex take him gently
from the midwife. He looks down adoringly at our son and
Finn falls silent. Alex glances over to me briefly, his eyes
shining with tears. My heart turns to butter.

Moments later, they repeat the procedure. I hear a pitiful cry and this time they hand little Faye to me. I hold her as best I can, with one arm under her and the other keeping her pulled in against me, tightly, while I lie flat on my back.

Wow. She's absolutely perfect. Her eyes are tightly shut. Her face is pink and wrinkled and she's sleeping peacefully. She looks like a tiny doll – just as cute as a button.

I will never let you go.

'Hello,' I say to my daughter for the very first time. I'm crying openly.

Alex and I have been blessed with a boy and a girl.

Bingo. We're chuffed to bits.

For the next few days, I'm in at the deep end. I have to learn the ropes very quickly. Alex continues to work as he needs to tie up a few loose ends before Christmas. I understand, but I'm bitterly disappointed that he doesn't stay for very long when he comes to visit us. On one occasion he only stays for an hour, because he is going straight out to wet the babies' heads with some of his friends. Meanwhile, I struggle with stitches, feeding and nappy changes, all on my own in the hospital. I'm upset that Alex spends so little time with us, but I don't have the confidence to challenge him. Then again, I never challenge Alex. I don't feel I have the right to challenge him. I'm not sure why I feel like that. More than likely, it's a lesson I've learned from my father.

Stay silent. Don't rock the boat.

But here I am, a new mother, with *two* babies, and I'm really struggling on my own in the hospital. Alex should be spending more time with the three of us and helping me out. With a defiance I haven't felt since childhood, I make a solemn promise to tell Alex exactly how I'm feeling.

But I never do. Not then, at least.

A few weeks after Finn and Faye are born, Penny gives birth to a beautiful baby girl with a shock of thick dark hair. Penny and Pete name her Felicity, but we all call her Fliss.

Penny and Fliss keep me sane in those early days. We push our prams to parks and coffee shops and we compare notes, while all three babies nap peacefully.

I envy them.

Every day, Alex returns from work, makes himself a cup of tea and goes straight outside to our little courtyard garden to smoke cannabis. I'm not at all happy about it, but still I say nothing.

Finn and Faye grow quickly. They're both happy, healthy babies, crawling at speed all over the house, while I struggle to keep up with them.

I never return to work. Alex and I decide that I'll stay at home and look after the children. We know that our finances will take a big hit once my maternity pay ends, but I have faith that we'll muddle through.

However, only a few months after receiving my final pay cheque, the financial strain begins to take its toll on Alex. I can see he needs a break – he has dark circles under his eyes for much of the time and he's constantly yawning and falling asleep on the sofa. The truth is, we could *both* do with a break. We sit down one evening and work out how we might get the four of us out to Barbados for a whole month. We decide to remortgage our house and blow the consequences. Finn and Faye are almost a year old now and something else is on my mind – I really want to introduce them both to their grandparents.

While I know that I'll never have the kind of mother-daughter relationship I long for – the kind I used to see as a child whenever I watched *The Waltons* or *Little House on the*

Prairie, Mum and I have, at least, managed to call a kind of truce in recent years. I hope she might treat me differently if she sees me as a mother in my own right. I hope she might be more like those mums on the TV.

How naïve I am.

On day two of our holiday in Barbados, we throw a party to celebrate Finn and Faye's first birthday, with brightly coloured pointy party hats, balloons, and horns that sound like sick geese. That makes us all laugh. Mum has baked a cake and my half-brother Mike has made a funny little clown out of a cardboard toilet roll holder, which sits rather lopsidedly on top of it. He's painted it with bright red and white stripes. I'm really touched by all their efforts.

Even my eldest half-brother Ray, is with us. Sober for now. Ray has come over from England and is now living with Dad in Barbados, helping him out with his map business. Mainly, I think it's an opportunity for Dad to keep a watchful eye on him.

My younger brother Casper, and his wife Sonia soon arrive. They introduce us to their seven-week-old daughter Bella. Mum seems delighted to have three grandchildren to fuss over. She's natural and sweet with Finn and Faye. I like watching how she is with them. But it doesn't last.

I've seen my mother for six days straight and I now want one day alone with Alex and the kids. Mum rings early and asks if she can come over with some soup, which she's made with leftover chicken.

'Thanks Mum, but can you bring it over tomorrow? Alex and I are going to go down to the beach with the kids.'

'I won't stay, Rachel. The soup is really delicious. I just want to drop it off.' I can hear a tone creeping into my mother's voice…determination.

'Sorry, Mum. We're leaving shortly. Let's speak tomorrow.' I'm holding my ground.

'I've been slaving over a hot stove since five o'clock this morning, Rachel. All I want to do is drop the soup off to you. Where's the problem?' She's now raising her voice.

'Mum, I haven't asked for any soup.' I'm now feeling a rush of adrenaline and a strong need to defend myself, from a history of injustice. I hate this feeling and I just want to get off the phone. 'I'm going now. I'll call you tomorrow.' I hang up. She calls straight back but I don't pick up. Alex does.

'Sorry, Carmen, we're just off to the beach now, but thanks for making us soup. I'll ask Rachel to call you tomorrow morning.' Alex is mouthing something to me but I can't quite understand. The grenade that is Mum finally explodes while poor Alex is trying desperately to get off the phone. I can actually hear Mum shouting as Alex holds the handset away from his ear.

Eventually, he puts the phone down with Mum's disjointed voice still screeching through the earpiece. He looks stunned.

'She called me an arsehole,' he says flatly.

'Oh,' is all I say. I'm right back where I always used to be as a child — with adrenaline coursing through my veins. I'm also embarrassed at the way my mother has spoken to Alex.

That is the last I hear from my mother until we are back at the airport three weeks later. In many ways I'm grateful for the peace, but guilt and a slow seeping sadness finally get the better of me. I call her a few days before we leave the island to ask her if she'll meet us at the airport to say goodbye.

'Mum, it's Rachel.' I say warily.

'Yes, Rachel. What is it?' she croaks. She sounds as if she's just woken up. It's late in the afternoon and I guess she's been napping.

'Mum, we're leaving on Friday. I want to say goodbye and I think it would be good if you saw the kids one more

time. I-I'm really not sure when we'll be back...' I'm finding
it difficult to say the words. They come tumbling out of my
mouth as if they don't belong to me. Despite my difficulty,
it feels like the right thing to do.

She agrees.

For our final few days on the island, Alex and I rent a
fabulously unspoiled wooden beach house over on the east
coast. It's perched high up on a ridge, painted yellow, and
green, with a wooden deck on three sides. We sit, mesmerised
by the rugged coastline sweeping away from us into the
distance. The sea on this side of the island is wild and rough; a
dark navy blue with crests of white. I watch the waves crashing
against the rocks and onto the wet sand far below. The sound
is carried on the Atlantic sea breeze, which rises up to meet us
as we sit out on the deck. It keeps us cool and sleepy.

Out of the blue, Alex jumps in the car to go and score some
weed. I don't stop him and I hate myself for saying nothing.
When he returns, I share his joint. I haven't been stoned for
almost two years. For the remainder of our holiday, the two of
us get high whenever the kids are napping indoors. I only wish
I was strong enough to say 'no,' because my paranoia returns
with a ferocity and a vengeance, which takes me by surprise.
It drags me back to a place I've almost forgotten. *Fear.*

I now find it very difficult to relax at night, as we're
completely isolated, in a pitch-black field at the end of a
long pot-holed dirt track. Every noise makes me jump. I'm
frightened. All over again.

Late one morning, a police car pulls up outside as Alex is
stubbing out a joint. The kids are napping inside and I'm
terrified, because we're both as high as kites.

Trying not to panic, I watch as the lone policeman gets out of his Land Rover, and I'm shocked to see that he's bare-chested. As he approaches us on the veranda, he pulls on a grey shirt and does up the buttons.

That's odd.

My mind is trying to work out what's going on. Perhaps the policeman lives nearby and the smell of cannabis has brought him up here. I'm relieved that he is friendly and his visit is brief. He leaves us with a warning to lock up securely at night. I look over at Alex as his Land Rover bounces away up the dirt track.

'That was close!' My heart is finally slowing down. 'What if he'd searched us?' I realise we're both too stoned to get into a discussion about it, but I doubt I would have said much more had I been lucid.

Ridiculously, I'm very glad to be driving away from that tranquil island paradise, because I no longer feel safe after the policeman's visit. It has nothing whatsoever to do with his warning, but everything to do with my growing paranoia.

At the airport, I see Mum approaching as we're standing in the check-in queue with all of our bags. I'm trying to keep Finn and Faye from wriggling out of my grasp and getting into mischief. I ignore the mammoth, which I see trailing heavily behind my mother; it won't do to mention the bloody soup now... or the last three weeks of stony silence.

Mum cuddles the children and we hug rather awkwardly as I say goodbye. She's subdued and I know instinctively that she wishes she'd spent more time with us. *I* wish she had. But I challenged her authority and the red mist descended. I was never allowed to make the rules. Not then. Not now.

It will be another fourteen years before she sees her grandchildren again.

CHAPTER 17

The following year, Alex and I are driving down to Cornwall with the kids asleep in the back. I've agreed to look after my sister's dog while she's away with her family for a fortnight. Philippa lives on the Lizard, very close to a beach, but we hardly ever leave her house. Mostly, it's because we're stoned. I want to stop smoking cannabis. *Desperately.* I never wanted to start again and this trip feels like the ideal time to broach the subject with Alex.

It's three o'clock in the morning and Finn begins to cry. This isn't at all unusual. Poor Finn suffers terribly with eczema and it often wakes him up at night. Thick with sleep, I get up and go to him. He must have been scratching his skin for some time as he's sitting up in his cot, and I can see his wrists are red raw and bleeding. I gently pick him up to comfort him, but what he needs is for the terrible itching to stop. I wipe his wrists and legs with a cool, damp flannel and then smother his legs and arms in cream before putting him back in his cot. It's a warm night and so I open the window to let in the air from outside. By now, Finn has settled back down and I'm grateful to be heading back to bed.

I'm just nodding off when Finn begins to cry again. I groan. Alex is fast asleep. He often sleeps when the kids are crying.

We've agreed to take it in turns to get up and so I nudge Alex gently.

'Alex. *Alex*,' I whisper. 'Finn's awake. I've just put cream on him, but he's woken up again.'

'He'll be fine, Rach. Just leave him for a bit,' Alex replies, sleepily. I feel a familiar knot of anger beginning to form in the pit of my stomach. Reluctantly, I leave Finn to cry for a while longer, to see if he'll settle back down on his own, but his cries grow louder and more persistent. By now, I'm wide awake.

'Alex, it's your turn to go!' I say, sharply. Without saying a word, he whips back the covers and stomps out of the room. I can hear him talking to Finn, who's immediately quiet. A few moments later, Alex is back in bed. He pulls the covers over himself aggressively and turns his back on me, saying nothing.

'Alex, I don't think we should be smoking cannabis anymore,' I say matter-of-factly. It just comes out. I surprise myself.

'What?' he snaps back at me in the dark. I repeat my words with a little less conviction this time. He sits up in bed. 'It's three in the bloody morning, Rach. I *don't* want to be talking about this now.'

It's my turn to sit up. 'Well, I *do*,' I hurl back at him.

Alex suddenly explodes. His fist comes flying out and connects with my jaw with a large crack.

I'm stunned. I can't close my mouth. My jaw is screaming in pain but I'm too shocked to speak. I back out of the bed and run out of the room, holding the side of my face.

'Rachel! Oh my God, *Rach*!'

I hear his voice behind me but I'm too terrified to stop. I run down to the kitchen in a panic, turning on all the lights. I push hard against my jaw and hear it click back into place. The pain is indescribable but at least I can close my mouth again.

Alex comes rushing into the kitchen. He is shocked and very scared. He seems small, despite his towering height. He stands directly across the kitchen table from me. I'm gripping the edge of the table to steady myself. The adrenaline has turned my legs to jelly and I'm breathing hard.

'Don't!' I shout in desperation, as he attempts to move around the table towards me. 'Alex, don't come any closer,' I beg, moving away. He stops.

'Rachel, I'm so sorry. I just don't know what happened. I-I lost it. I'm so, *so* sorry. God…' He bursts into tears, sinking onto the floor like a condemned tower block in a controlled explosion. All six foot four of him lands in an untidy heap. He puts his head in his hands. His huge shoulders are hunched over and he's sobbing uncontrollably.

Almost immediately, without Alex saying one word, I forgive him. I'm oblivious to the solid fist of resentment that takes root inside of me at the very same time.

I always knew Alex had an explosive temper. His friends had mentioned several occasions when Alex lost control, although I never actually witnessed it myself. I learned very early on in our relationship when to leave Alex alone, recognising when he's angry – he looks directly at me without saying a word, silently smouldering until I look away. This is my cue to either change the subject or leave him alone. Oddly enough, it is *exactly* the same feeling I had around my mother. I was intimidated by her.

The realisation hits me like a slap in the face. This is history repeating itself. Only, I can see Alex's remorse. He is inconsolable. On unsteady legs, I walk over to him and lower myself to the floor. Sitting on the cool kitchen tiles, I hold him in my arms until his sobs subside, like a baby. Neither of us says another word.

Eventually, we go back upstairs and climb into bed, exhausted. I'm not going to go back to sleep. I know that – my jaw is hurting like hell. I lie on my back, staring up at the ceiling. My mind is replaying the shocking events of the night, over and over again.

I feel partly to blame. I knew we were both short on sleep and stressed because of Finn's crying. I should never have picked that time in the morning to speak to Alex about our cannabis addiction.

Only a short while later, Faye's gentle cry brings me back to the reality that the day has already begun. I look over at Alex. He's sleeping soundly. I don't care. I'm too weary to care. Exhaustion and misery cling to my body, seeping deep into my bones, as I get up and walk into the children's bedroom.

I neither have the courage nor the will to talk to Alex after that. He continues to smoke cannabis and I do, too.

Once again, I'm addicted. And the tar-black monster has moved in for good.

I only feel safe with Penny. We spend a lot of time together as the children grow up. I hardly see Connie anymore. She and Evan decide not to have children. They discover the London party scene instead and make new friends... friends who are equally unencumbered by parental responsibilities.

As if things aren't bad enough, events spiral out of control when Alex discovers skunk – just about the strongest strain of cannabis available.

It blows my head off.

If I thought I was paranoid before, smoking skunk amplifies my feelings tenfold.

Alex loves it.

I *hate* it.

And my resentment towards him grows.

During this time, Alex's student friends are frequent visitors. When they're not away at university, they come over specifically to smoke cannabis with Alex – while Finn and Faye are sleeping peacefully upstairs. This makes me feel very angry. Alex is putting his friends before Finn and Faye's health. When his friends aren't visiting, Alex and I usually smoke outside in our courtyard garden, or we sit in the fireplace and smoke up the chimney.

One evening, after Alex's student friends have left, I finally pluck up the courage to talk to him about it.

'Alex, I really don't want your friends using our place as a doss house.' Almost inevitably, we begin to argue. Suddenly, Alex picks up a kitchen knife and he starts to gouge chunks of wood out of our kitchen worktop. He's completely out of control. *Will he attack me?*

I want to flee from the house, but I'm going nowhere – there's absolutely no way I'm leaving the kids alone upstairs. Not with Alex like that. Shaking like a leaf, I plead with him to calm down.

'Hun, *please*.' I face him, terrified. He's sweating heavily. The knife flashes in the kitchen light. He looks at it in his hand and seems confused. I watch his anger dissipating with each heaving breath. There are splinters of wood all over the tiled floor.

He puts the knife down carefully and looks back at me, fear and confusion in his eyes. I don't think he knows what just happened and I can see that he's frightened by what he's done to the worktop. He runs his fingers over the gouges in the wood again and again. I'm watching him in slow motion as he slides his index finger up and down and then sideways, along and across the grooves. Is this helping him remember? In that precise moment, I know with every fibre of my being that something terrible has just been averted.

I take the knife very carefully from Alex, put it back in the block and leave the kitchen. Moments later, I can hear him on the telephone, speaking to the Samaritans. I can't quite catch what he's saying, but he's deeply upset. His voice breaks several times.

I'm much too afraid to challenge Alex about smoking cannabis after that night. More sinister, however, is the very real fear that begins to take root in my mind — that Alex might actually kill me one day.

I know I have to stop smoking cannabis, but I'm going to have to go it alone. It won't be at all easy, because I'm addicted – not physically, but mentally. I'm addicted to the very brief release, which takes me away from all the stress in my life – stress that is mostly, ironically, created *because* of the cannabis. It's been a very long time since the days when I naïvely believed that cannabis was harmless. I'm seriously struggling to cope with life and there is no more length left in my tether. Something has to change.

I dig deeper than I've ever done before and I quit. I'm absolutely determined to show Alex that I'm serious and I know he won't take me seriously if I continue to smoke cannabis with him. Why would he?

Almost a month passes. It's enough time for me to feel clear-headed and brave enough to broach the subject with Alex, once again.

'Alex, I really need to talk to you.' My heart begins to beat rapidly and my mouth is now dry.

'What's up, Rach?' He's in the process of rolling a joint.

'Alex, I really want you to stop smoking cannabis. *Please*. I don't want it in our lives anymore. I don't want it in *my* life anymore.' There is a lump forming inside my throat as I speak. I'm very close to tears.

Alex stops what he's doing with the open joint in his two hands. He looks up at me without blinking. A challenge. I'm more than used to him staring me out. Only this time, I don't look away. I stare right back at him, calmly, until I see an almost imperceptible jolt in his body – an acknowledgment that this exchange is somehow different... that *I* am somehow different. He looks down at his hands, but he continues to roll the joint, despite the obvious change in energy between us. This proves to be a major turning point in our relationship.

The next day, I tell Alex to find somewhere else to live while he cleans up his act. Perhaps to his step-parents', Robert and Beth? I suggest we have a trial separation so Alex can come to terms with what I'm asking of him. The truth is, I don't want Alex around me or the kids while he's withdrawing from cannabis, because I'm frightened he might lose it again.

Reluctantly, he agrees. Perhaps a little too easily. He makes a phone call, packs a bag and leaves. I'm very disappointed when I find out that he's moved in with a friend of his from Brighton – a friend who smokes one hell of a lot of cannabis.

Alex has been gone for almost three weeks when our new neighbour, John, knocks on the door. John is a plumber and we met for the first time only a few weeks ago when he began talking to Alex over the garden wall, offering him some private work.

'Rachel, hi. Is Alex in? I've got another job for him.'

'Er, no. He's not,' I reply, self-consciously. 'He's, er, staying with a friend at the moment but he'll be on his mobile...'

My voice trails off as I hear Faye crying. A wave of self-pity washes over me at the way John is looking at me.

'You know I've also got twins,' he says, sympathetically. I glance back into the house, still holding the door. 'They're nineteen now.' He laughs, understandingly. 'Let me know if there's anything you need, eh?' he says, with his head cocked to one side. I thank him and close the door.

My feathers are ruffled and from that moment on, I become acutely aware of John's presence on the other side of the wall. I hear his TV. I hear him talking on the phone. I hear him moving about inside his house. I can actually *see* him in his kitchen whenever I'm standing at the sink in mine.

As time passes, I become obsessed with him. I have absolutely no idea why. John is much older than me and he's not my type. I think the fact he's kind to me means so much more during those lonely days without Alex.

Alex and I come to an arrangement that he'll visit the children at least once a week. I'm emptying the dishwasher when he calls out from the hallway the first time. Finn and Faye stop what they're doing and immediately run off to find him. I can hear them jumping up and down on the wooden floorboards, begging to be picked up. I catch up with them in time to see Alex swinging them up easily, one in each arm, to give them both a big squeeze.

'I missed you buddy,' he says to Finn, suddenly serious. 'And you, princess.' He turns to Faye, who giggles back at him. It breaks my heart seeing the three of them together like this.

My family. Normality.

I waver as Alex disappears out of the front door to take them out. When he returns, I offer him a cup of tea. We've hardly spoken since he's left and I'm keen to know if he's still smoking skunk.

'I'm doing my best, Rach. I've cut down *a lot*. Believe me. I'll get there, hun, I promise.'

My heart sinks. Looking after the children on my own is exhausting and I'm really struggling. I know it's only a matter of time before I hit the wall.

As it turns out, John prevents that from happening. He calls around the following day to see if I'm ok, and this time, I burst into tears. He pushes past me and takes me by the hand, leading me into our sitting room.

'Wait there,' he says with a look of concern in his eyes. Moments later, he's back with a cup of tea. John is lovely to me and I'm eternally grateful for his kindness – and for his attention.

Much later, that cup of tea turns into a glass of wine, and then another, and in a crazy moment of weakness, I cross an invisible line.

It feels very strange kissing another man after so many years, but I don't care if what I'm doing is wrong. It's been a very long time since I've had any kind of intimacy or even an interesting conversation with another man. Alex is always too stoned to talk to me. Suddenly, I feel alive and I want more.

A week later, Alex is back, asking if he can move back in.
Does he know?

He assures me he's finally quit smoking cannabis and I believe him. I'm also conflicted because of recent events with John. However, I'm not ready to give up on my marriage. Not by a mile. I've really missed having Alex around and that surprises me. Finn and Faye have missed him, too. Before the end of the day, Alex is back with his bags. Back where he belongs.

It feels like a fresh start. Almost. I can hear John talking on the phone through our sitting room wall. The sound is muffled, but I'm immediately overwhelmed with guilt. It won't do to have him so close while I'm trying to get my marriage back on track.

I persuade Alex to put our house up for sale.

CHAPTER 18

As luck would have it, Alex and I manage to sell our house in less than two weeks. During that time, we find a pretty whitewashed cottage to rent in a nearby village. It's a relief when we finally leave our house for the very last time.

A year later, we move again, to another rented property, so that Finn and Faye can attend the very same primary school I once lived next door to back when I was dating Ben.

Finn is wearing smart grey shorts while Faye is spinning around in her grey flannel skirt. They're each wearing a white short-sleeved shirt with the school logo on it and both have bright red caps on their heads. Finn beams at me with a toothy smile as they jostle for best position while I attempt to take their photograph. Finally, I capture the moment – an image that will remain forever with me. Their very first day of school.

I drive away with a lump in my throat and tears streaming down my face. I feel a little ridiculous, but already I miss them terribly. The house is deathly quiet as I close the front door behind me. It takes me a long time to get used to that silence.

With the kids now at school, it feels like the right time for us to be putting down roots again. Alex seems relieved when I suggest a more permanent move, and within a few short weeks, we've bought our second home. It's much larger than our previous house, with a huge garden for the kids to run around in. The interior is drab, dated and in desperate need of updating, but that doesn't bother me. It has bags of potential. Almost immediately, we set to work stripping the walls.

We've been living in our new house for only three weeks and I'm outside in my slippers, emptying the bin, late one Saturday morning. Just then, Alex pulls into the drive in his large blue van. Finn and Faye are laughing together in the front seat. Alex has taken them both out so I can have a lie in. Finn sticks his head out of the window.

'Mummy, look what Daddy has in his van!' He's holding something out in his hand. I close the wheelie bin and walk over as Alex opens his door and jumps out. He's smiling broadly at me, not in the least bit perturbed.

'Oh, dear. Rumbled.' He laughs. Faye is leaning forward inside the van, picking something up from a small box on the dashboard.

'Sugar lumps,' she cries, popping a white sugary square into her mouth. Her eyes grow wide as she closes her mouth around it. Finn briefly shows me the sugar lump in his hand before it disappears the same way as Faye's. Alex looks at me a little sheepishly.

'Sorry, babe, they found my stash. They've had quite a few, I'm afraid.' He laughs again, but I don't care. It's great seeing them all so happy. He walks around to the near side of his van, opens the door and leans inside to release Finn and then Faye from their seat belts. There are two booster seats in the front of his van, permanently. The kids love their outings in Alex's van as the front seats are so high up and they can both easily see out of the large windscreen.

Like a well-rehearsed performance, Alex swings Finn and then Faye high up into the air with both arms, before bringing them down to stand squarely back on their feet on the brick-paved drive. They screech with delight and run past me into the house.

'Did you get any more sleep?' He leans in and plants a kiss fully on my mouth.

'I did. Thanks.' I smile back at him gratefully. I'm happy to have them all home again. I follow the kids back into the house. *Our house.*

I only wish I'd savoured the happiness I felt that day and the fragile hope I'd been clinging to ever since we moved in – hope that Alex and I would be ok this time. However, like a delicate wine glass slipping through my fingers, it wasn't long before my dream of a brand-new start was shattered into a million pieces.

A few days later, Alex comes home from work, makes himself a cup of tea and takes the mug out to the shed to have with a cigarette. I'm clearing away the kids' supper plates when I suddenly remember that Alex's sister Dot, called earlier and she's due to ring again.

'Shit,' I wipe my hands on a tea towel and snatch the phone out of its cradle to take outside to Alex. Almost immediately, I detect a faint smell of cannabis drifting across the garden. I open the shed door in time to see Alex inhaling deeply on a perfectly rolled joint.

'Alex?' I gasp in shock. 'What the *hell* are you doing?' My world comes crashing down like a house of cards.

'Babe, I'm sorry, I just can't cope at the moment. I really can't. Hun, *please*. Don't be mad.' He looks at me with utter desperation and for the very first time, I can actually see the pain, raw and unrelenting, in his eyes. Like a dark chasm with no walls – it terrifies me. How have I never noticed this before? Naïvely, I've been living in a bubble of self-denial, thinking that everything is ok and, just like that, it bursts. Without saying a word, I turn and walk back to the house with my heart on the floor.

That night, after the kids have gone to bed, Alex and I speak together in whispers. He admits he's been feeling bad for weeks. He seems lost.

'Alex, why don't you talk to someone? Get some professional help?'

'Rachel, I can't. I just can't.' He's hunched over in a ball. I'm looking at a broken man. Alex convinces me that he needs cannabis to stop him from losing his mind. Without it, he's absolutely terrified. I can see the demons are hot on his tail, and right then, I probably would have agreed to anything.

'Alex, ok, but I really want you to go and talk to someone. Let me find someone for you to talk to. Please. At least do this for the kids, will you?' I put my hand on his leg and squeeze. He nods, a small movement with potentially huge implications for all of us.

Our agreement was only ever meant to be a temporary bridge to get Alex out of a dark hole. I was unaware that my resolve was also hanging, just as precariously, by the finest of threads.

Only a few days later, I go outside to find Alex in the shed in order to discuss whether we can afford for me to go away for a few days with Penny and Connie. I sit down next to him on our old tea-stained sofa. The broken springs creak under my weight. The shed is thick with smoke and almost immediately, I'm a little lightheaded, and I like the feeling very much. I've missed it. Without thinking, I take the joint out of Alex's hands, put the end of it in my mouth and inhale the smoke deep into my lungs.

Alex doesn't stop me. He just looks at me with a mixture of surprise and relief — the relief of a fellow addict. He's off the hook and I've fallen off the wagon. *I hate myself.*

In no time at all, we're smoking cannabis together in the evenings, and sooner still, we return to the stony silence of our unhappy marriage.

Less than two weeks later, Penny, Connie and I are sunbathing on the whitewashed roof of a kasbah in the heart of Marrakesh. The sun is beating down on my skin. The scent of exotic spices fills the air and, suddenly, my problems back in England seem very far away.

I don't ever want to go back.

We're discussing Alex and my frustration that we're both smoking cannabis again.

'Rach, you can't smoke it with him and expect him to stop. That's double standards. You've got to stop smoking it yourself and he'll know you mean business,' Penny says, matter-of-factly, as she applies another layer of suntan lotion to her already tanned legs.

'Why on earth did you start again?' Connie turns over onto her front and shoots me a disapproving look. I can smell Penny's expensive sun cream; it's thick and sweet in the air.

'Because I'm an arse...' my voice trails away, 'and I have absolutely no willpower. Alex smokes it all day, *every* day. It's right there in front of my face.' I'm immediately defensive, but I know they're both right. Their perspective seems obvious and I suppose I need to have it spelled out. Mostly, I need to hear someone else saying those words. Talking things through with Penny and Connie finally gives me the courage to do something about it.

When I get back from that holiday, I quit again. Just like that.

Almost immediately, I can see the fear in Alex's eyes when he realises that I'm no longer going outside to the shed with him in the evenings. He says nothing but he knows what's coming next.

I try several times to pick my moment but, in the end, I can't face going through it all again with him. Instead, I stay up after Alex has gone to bed and write him a letter:

Dear Alex,

I'm so sorry but I can't go on like this anymore. It feels like we're a million miles apart again. I hate what cannabis is doing to us and, Alex, I'm scared of you. That's no way for a wife to feel about her husband. I'm terrified of how you'll react if I bring this up but I can't keep quiet anymore because it's killing me. Please, please will you get some help to quit smoking cannabis once and for all? If not, I'm going to leave but you need to know I'll be taking Finn and Faye with me. It's just not right for them to be around drugs. Deep down, I know you understand that being stoned all the time isn't right for them or us.

Alex, I am here for you but we need to get past this horrible place where we both are right now and I can't do this on my own. I really need your help. Please.

Rachel

x

I leave the letter propped up against the kettle and I go upstairs to bed.

The following morning, it's gone. My mind is in turmoil for the entire day, knowing that he's read it. *What is he thinking?*

Will he be angry with me? He doesn't call and I don't have the courage to ring him at work to talk about it. I'm terrified of what he might say, or do.

By the time he pulls into the drive later that afternoon, I've worried myself to the point that I think I might actually be sick. I watch him getting out of his van through the kitchen window. The blinds clatter together noisily as I peer through a small gap with trembling fingers. My heart is hammering away inside my chest.

I hear Alex wiping his feet noisily on the mat as I cower in the kitchen. I have no idea what to expect. He walks in and our eyes meet. I can see he's as frightened as me. He walks over and takes my hands in his.

'Sorry…' His voice breaks, 'Rachel, I'm *so* sorry.'

The relief I feel is palpable and I almost crumple to the floor. I need to sit down, quickly. My legs have turned to jelly.

Just then, Finn shouts from the living room. 'Daddy!' He comes running in, followed by Faye.

'Let's talk later.' I force a smile and plonk myself down heavily onto one of the kitchen stools. It wobbles precariously under my weight. I don't want to have a discussion in front of the kids. Alex looks at me and nods in agreement. Seconds later, he's striding out of the kitchen, followed by an excited Finn and Faye. I hear them laughing together in the sitting room – a strangely alien sound, given the way I feel.

That night, after the kids have gone to bed, Alex and I finally have a proper heart-to-heart.

'Rachel, I know things need to change. I understand how you feel and I'm scared, too.' He looks at me briefly and then back down at his feet. He's sitting cross-legged on the floor, with his back against one of our distressed leather sofas. His hands are folded loosely in his lap and he's tapping his thumbs together, restlessly. I'm sitting directly opposite him on a large wing-back chair picking at the frayed brocade around one of the arms. It's not my chair – I'm looking after it for Robyn – but I like to sit here in the evenings. I look across at Alex. We've been here before and I'm not sure how best to reply.

'Finn and Faye will be six in a few weeks. I don't want them growing up thinking that being stoned is normal. I don't want them to think it's ok.' I sigh deeply.

Groundhog Day.

'Rachel, honestly, it's not a big deal. If you really feel like that, you know I'll stop. I can take it or leave it.' He flashes me a look, more defiant than conciliatory. He seems irritated that I'm making him address something that I know, deep down, he wants to carry on doing.

'Alex, if you really think you can leave it, then I think it's more than about time you do. I don't want cannabis in our lives anymore. I really *don't*. Why not let me call someone and maybe you can talk to them? Get some proper support?'

'No, it's ok.' He's adamant. 'Rachel, if it means this much to you, I'll stop. I promise. I won't buy any more and I promise you, I won't smoke any more. Ok?' He looks at me again and this time I see a flicker of desperation. I don't believe him and I'm not entirely sure he believes himself. 'I don't want to lose you, Rach. Or the kids. You know that.'

This conversation has been five long years in the making, this silent showdown, and I've already had my fill of words. What I need is action.

'Ok. It's ok, hun. You won't lose me.' I get up and sit down next to him on the floor. I reach out and put one arm around his huge shoulders, pulling him in towards me. He seems like a small child, this enormous hulk of a man. Alex buries his head in his hands and his body begins to convulse in wave after wave of silent sobs.

Right then, the resentment I've been holding onto disappears completely and the lump inside my throat finally dislodges. Tears spill over and run silently down my face. They land on Alex's knee.

How on earth did we get here?

The next afternoon after work, Alex drives down to the coast to join his two best friends for an evening of beach fishing. I'm aware that they both smoke cannabis and curious about his decision to put himself so quickly in the way of temptation. However, I'm fast asleep by the time he climbs into bed later that night.

The following morning, over breakfast, I ask him about his evening. He knows exactly what I mean.

'I-I had a smoke on the beach. Just one, Rach…' He's looking at me intently, trying to gauge my reaction.

I stand up from the breakfast bar, almost spilling my tea, and storm out of the kitchen. I feel like screaming.

I don't trust myself to have a conversation with Alex. I'm torn between a sense of hopeless futility and raw fury. It's a dangerous, claustrophobic mix. I lock myself in the bathroom and perch on the lid of the toilet, looking around in desperation and breathing hard. I want to bite down hard on something, *anything*, to relieve the pressure building up inside me.

Alex knocks on the door. Once. I don't reply. Instead, I lean over to the sink and I turn the cold tap on full to drown out the noise of everything else around me, especially the pounding inside my ears. I need Alex to leave. Eventually, he does.

All day, Alex tries to call me, but I refuse to pick up the phone. When he finally arrives back home, I'm sitting with

Finn and Faye in the kitchen as they eat their supper. He walks in with flowers in one hand and a tray of sushi in the other. It's a peace offering. I don't care.

I turn away, completely ignoring him. Anger rises up from my belly. My heart is already racing.

'Rach, please.'

Nothing. Silent rage.

Eventually, he gives up trying to talk to me altogether. He marches upstairs instead, slamming our bedroom door behind him. I finish clearing up the kitchen and I go and quarter-fill the bath for Finn.

Once Finn has finished bathing and is in his pyjamas, I help Faye into the bath and I go upstairs to talk with Alex. I find him sitting on the floor next to the bed, in tears. I feel cold and detached, but beneath this I am very, very angry.

'Alex, Faye is in the bath and I really need you to take over.' My voice is flat. I hardly recognise it. Alex is inconsolable, but I remain unmoved. I sit down on the edge of the bed and wait for him to reply. There is a fist of fire growing inside me, deep in the pit of my stomach.

'Look at me, Rachel. I can't. *I just can't.*' His voice breaks as he holds out both hands, palms up and fingers spread. It suddenly dawns on me that I'm looking down at a boy. A small boy.

Despite this, I'm struggling to see past my own anger. I'm battling hard to keep it down. I can't get past the fact that Alex went back on his promise. I can't believe that his resolve lasted for less than one day... that he chose cannabis over us.

'How do you expect me to be, Alex? I'm your wife!' I get up and walk back downstairs to help Faye out of the bath.

And that's when my whole world implodes.

I'm in the bathroom with Faye when Alex comes thundering down the stairs. Something has flipped inside of him. Suddenly, I am very, *very* frightened.

Finn is in the next room playing a game on the sofa and Faye has just got out of the bath. She's standing next to me with a towel wrapped around her, looking at me intently. The bathroom door is slightly ajar. I'm rooted to the spot, holding my breath.

I don't know what to do.

Alex is now in the kitchen and I can just see the back of him. He picks up the flowers and hurls them into the bin. For a very brief moment he disappears from view, then returns with the tray of sushi, which he throws aggressively on top of the flowers. He lifts his foot up and brings it down hard inside the bin, stamping over and over and smashing everything inside to a pulp.

I want to grab the kids and get the hell out of there, but I can't move. The knife rack is inches away from Alex and I'm praying he won't see it. Instead, he turns and runs straight back upstairs, slamming the bedroom door behind him. I can hear him crashing around, through the ceiling directly above me. He's in our walk-in loft.

What the hell is he doing?

Finally, I find the courage to move. I help Faye to dress as quickly as I can, but it's not at all easy, because my fingers are shaking so much.

Three loud thuds come from upstairs. *Boom. Boom. Boom.*

I need to check what's going on. My heart is in my mouth. I walk up the stairs and try the bedroom door. It's locked. A strange feeling settles over me. Cold. Silent. Something is very wrong. My instincts are telling me to leave the house. *Immediately.*

I can't explain this feeling, because I've never felt anything like it before. I only know that I have to leave. *Right now.*

I run back downstairs and find the children standing at the bottom of the stairs, their eyes like saucers. I grab their coats and the three of us leave. Finn and Faye are still in their pyjamas.

I'm driving around aimlessly — I've turned down the same road three times and driven around in a loop — back to the very same spot. I don't know where to go or what to do.

Breathe, Rachel.

I have my mobile phone with me.

Call Deborah.

Deborah is another mum from Finn and Faye's school. She lives only a few hundred metres away and she already knows a lot about Alex and me.

'Deb, it's Rachel. I'm really sorry to bother you, but I don't know what else to do. Alex is in a state and I'm really scared.' My voice wavers. I'm on the brink of tears.

'Oh, my God, Rachel. Come straight over.' She sounds shocked.

I probably look as if I've seen a ghost, standing with Finn and Faye in their pyjamas, on Deborah's doorstep. She beckons the three of us inside. I follow her into the kitchen where she offers me a cup of tea. Deborah's oldest daughter takes Finn and Faye upstairs to find her other children.

In the meantime, I tell Deborah everything that's happened. She listens to me intently without saying one word. When I finish talking, she offers to drive over to my house with her husband and check on Alex, while I stay put with the kids. I agree.

My mind is in a spin, playing over the events of the evening. *What's happened to Alex? What will Deborah and her husband find?* My heart is beating so fast, I'm struggling to catch my breath.

Suddenly, my mobile phone rings, making me jump out of my skin. I spill tea all over my lap. The tea is stone cold. I'm shaking so much that, at first, I can't answer the call.

'Rachel!' Deborah is shouting. I can hear panic rising in her voice. 'Tom has broken down your bedroom door. We've found Alex. Rachel, I've called an ambulance and Sasha is on her way over to you.'

Sasha is another friend of ours from the school. She also knows about Alex and me.

'What? Deb? Is Alex ok?' My voice is barely more than a whisper, but Deborah refuses to say any more.

'Rachel, I-I've got to go. It's ok. He's ok…' The line goes dead. My blood runs cold. I know that Alex is not ok.

I hear an ambulance passing by on the road outside.

It's going to my house.

Just then, there's a knock at Deborah's front door. Suddenly, everything feels strange. I'm confused. My heart is beating so rapidly, I feel faint. I get up and answer the door on unsteady legs. *I'm in a dream.* It's Sasha.

'Sasha, what's happened? Please. Tell me…' My voice trails off at the expression on her face.

She is looking back at me, terrified. Her mouth is forming words. Shapes, with no sound. She pauses, takes a deep shuddering breath, and then gently takes both of my hands in hers. Her fingers are cold. She's trembling. She looks up at me, directly into my eyes.

'Dear God, Rachel. I'm so, *so* sorry. Alex is dead.'

CHAPTER 19

My legs refuse to work. I've seen it happen on the TV, when mothers with sons in the forces get that dreaded knock at the door and can no longer stand up – I know how that feels.

While my brain is doing its very best to take in what Sasha is saying, shock cuts off the messages travelling down my spine to my legs. I crumple to the floor.

The police arrive shortly afterwards. They endeavour to take a statement from me. The sweet, gentle policewoman takes her time while I struggle to process the reality of Alex's death and recount everything that happened before the children and I fled from the house. I still have absolutely no idea how Alex has died and I won't allow anyone to tell me. All I know is that Alex has taken his own life. *I don't want to know how.*

Deborah calls my sister in Cornwall and Philippa and her husband Patrick, drive over five hours through the night to pick me and the children up. In the meantime, Deborah returns to my house to put a few things in a bag for the three of us, while I brief Finn and Faye in what begins to feel like a military operation. I feel numb. *Keep going.*

'We're going on holiday. Philippa and Patrick are on their way to pick us up right now,' I say, with a forced smile plastered on my face. Finn and Faye are immediately excited. Their reaction seems bizarre to me. I've stepped into a strange dream world and nothing makes any sense. *Stay strong, Rachel. Stay strong.*

We are back in Cornwall by lunchtime and I haven't slept, nor have Philippa or Patrick. We are utterly exhausted. It's the first of many nights when sleep will evade me.

I feel oddly detached from everything around me. It's impossible to take everything in.

Alex is dead.

The birds are singing sweetly in the trees outside my window and I can hear the traffic passing by on the road outside Philippa's house. Normal life. While everything in my life is very far from normal.

It takes everything in my power not to panic. I want to scream at the top of my lungs. I walk over to the mirror in my sister's spare room. My skin is greyish-white and I have dark circles under both eyes.

I keep wondering how Alex died. I imagine him with his wrists slashed open. I see him lying in a pool of blood, with his life slowly ebbing away. I can't bear to think about it. *Could I have prevented Alex's death? Should I have called the police straightaway?*

This is torture.

The truth is, for a split second, I'd thought about calling the police, but I didn't want to betray Alex by admitting to them that I was calling because I was frightened for my life.

I push the thought away and go and sit in the garden.

Finn and Faye still have no idea their father is dead and I'm too frightened to tell them. Neither of them has asked where Alex is and I'm thankful for that, at least. I'm terrified of the impact his death is going to have on them. I want to wrap them up and keep them safe.

How do I tell them? How does a mother tell her children that their father is dead? I put it off for another day. I simply can't face it.

The next morning dawns sunny and bright in Cornwall. I've only slept for an hour or two and I feel horrible.

I have to tell them. Today.

I'm lying in bed, looking up at the ceiling. An awful feeling of dread is writhing around inside my stomach, like a pit of snakes. It's been there from the moment I learned of Alex's death, steadily growing in intensity.

'Please, please help me.' I whisper a prayer.

Suddenly, I know what to do.

Philippa drives us to a small car park perched high up on a cliff only a few minutes away. We know it very well and, from here, I can clearly see the beach below us. We spent many summers here over the years.

At the rear of the beach, sand gives way to tall brown tufts of grass, which butt up to the edge of the clipped, lush greens of a links golf course. The beach itself is relatively small and, on this side, the rock rises up majestically to meet the footpath at the very top of the cliff, where we are standing with the crisp winter wind whipping hair into our eyes. The roof of a small stone church can just be seen on the opposite side of the beach below us.

This is the place.

We make our way slowly down the craggy path and out onto the sand. My sister holds back as I continue to walk further down the beach with Finn and Faye. I stop halfway and sit, patting the sand on either side of me, indicating that I want the children to sit down next to me. I'm mesmerised by the large grey swell of the sea. To the left of the bay, huge waves crash noisily against the rocks, shooting spray high up into the air. This world is wild and untamed.

My life feels like this.

I gather every last ounce of courage I can muster, take a deep breath and begin to speak in a calm, level tone.

'Finn. Faye. Daddy is dead.' I look at them both and then back at the waves in front of me. 'He won't be coming back.'

'How, Mum? How did he die?' Finn asks. I'm deeply grateful that I don't have to lie, because I still have no idea. Not yet, at least.

'I don't know,' I almost whisper, shaking my head. Faye is very quiet, but I know she's taking it all in. She watches the waves break in front of us and then looks from me to the sea, and then back again.

'Can we still speak to him on the phone?' Finn asks, seriously – something they both enjoyed whenever I used to call Alex at work.

'No, darling,' I reply, with a heart of lead, 'but we don't need a phone to talk to him where he is. If you speak to him, he will still hear you.' Finn looks at me and cocks his head to one side. Faye is now looking intently at Finn, waiting for his response.

'Mum, can I go and play now?' he asks, innocently. And with that, the knot in my stomach evaporates like frozen mist on a warm summer breeze. I breathe a huge sigh of relief.

Finn and Faye get up and run to dip their feet in the water. They squeal with delight as their shoes disappear under the frothy white foam. They poke their little fingers into tiny holes that form as the sand bubbles beneath the retreating waves.

We're going to be ok. I squeeze my eyes shut for a few brief seconds and then turn around and give my sister a thumbs-up.

Philippa and Patrick handle all the funeral arrangements, checking in with me from time to time to ask me exactly what I want. Flower. Hymns.

Coffin.

They scoop me up and make me feel safe when the world around me feels frightening and strange. They shield me away from my terrible reality. I will never, ever forget their unwavering kindness.

We return for Alex's funeral in less than a week. Alex's closest friends and family gather at the service to say goodbye.

I've written a speech – it feels vitally important for me to speak about Alex at the funeral – because no one really understands why he took his own life, least of all me. Despite all our difficulties, I want everyone to know that Alex was an incredibly loving and devoted father. I also want everyone to remember the good times, because we all had plenty of those.

When they bring Alex in, with his closest friends as pallbearers, his coffin seems much too small – he was so tall in life. *I wonder if he's really in there?* I want to ask others if they're thinking the same thing. Instead, I take a deep breath and focus on the enormous wreath of fragrant white flowers placed neatly on the top of his coffin. *May the bad times forever be forgotten.* I pray silently as Alex lies in a casket a few feet away from me.

It's my turn to speak. I stand up, walk slowly up to the podium and clear my throat. All I can see is a sea of faces, which fills the space, spilling out through the doors at the back of the room, where others are listening through speakers outside.

I recognise Jim's face in particular, standing right in front of me. Jim is one of my longest-standing male friends; the only black face among a sea of white; deeply spiritual, with one foot firmly placed in the next world. Something about his expression gives me the strength to make it through to the end of my speech. I remain composed until the curtains draw around Alex's coffin. I know what happens next.

Finally, my tears come.

After the funeral, Finn, Faye and I are driven back to Penny's house. I'm not ready to go back home yet, and Penny and Pete have invited the three of us to stay with them for as long as we want. I'm deeply grateful to have a few days to transition as my world recalibrates.

Will I ever adjust?

Almost a week after the funeral, Penny drives me home. I'm finally ready to learn how Alex died, and Penny thinks it's best to tell me when we're back at the house. She has already learned all the details of that terrible night from Deborah and her husband, and she asks me to trust her.

My hands are trembling so much that I struggle to put the key in the front door lock. Tick, tick, tick. Brass against brass. Penny takes the key from me gently and, without saying a word, puts it in the lock and pushes the door open for me. I take a deep breath, look at her briefly and step back into the house.

Everything is exactly as I left it. I can actually feel the silence. It smells like home, although I can detect a very faint trace of linseed oil. We both look around and then walk upstairs. I follow Penny into my bedroom, aware of a pulse throbbing, quick and strong, at my temples.

Oh, God.

Nothing is out of place. The only difference I can see is the glass panel on the bedroom door has been replaced. Unpainted putty, long since hardened, surrounds the new pane of frosted glass. The pattern is new. Penny tells me that

Deborah's husband broke the glass so that he could reach through and open the door from the inside, when they were looking for Alex. Stewart, a friend of Alex's, came over right away and replaced the panel, as soon as he heard what had happened. The bedroom is otherwise unchanged.

'How does it feel in here, Rach?' Penny asks, gently. I breathe in and think for a moment.

'It feels, um, *normal*.'

Penny asks if I'm ready to hear what happened. I nod, slowly. My heart is pumping fast, but I know I can't keep running away from the truth. It's time for me to learn exactly what happened to Alex.

Penny takes a deep breath and begins to tell me.

Alex ran back upstairs, slammed the door and locked it.

That much, I already know.

Next, he went through into the walk-in loft next to our bedroom. It was here that I assumed he killed himself, because I was in the bathroom directly beneath him with Faye when I heard all the banging going on above me. When Sasha told me Alex was dead, I immediately thought Alex had cut his wrists. But he hadn't.

The reason that Alex was banging around in the loft was because he was searching for a ligature. When he found what he was looking for, he returned to the bedroom, tied one end of nylon rope around our bedhead, the other end around his neck, and then he jumped out of the window.

Suddenly, the sound comes back to me.

Boom. Boom. Boom.

While Penny is talking, I break out in goosebumps. I can feel them in my hair. The noise I heard was Alex's body hitting the outside wall of our house. Three times. Followed by a deathly silence. That silence chilled me to the bone.

Everything falls into place as I put all of the pieces together. Penny is watching me intently.

'He didn't die in the house...' I whisper, my voice trailing off.

'No,' Penny replies, 'he didn't.'

Knowing that Alex hadn't cut his wrists and bled to death while I was having a cup of tea with Deborah is a peculiar kind of relief. I've been blaming myself ever since Alex's death for not doing something sooner. I've been consumed with guilt, but now I know there was nothing I could have done to save him.

Right then, something else strikes me – Finn was sitting on the sofa directly opposite the living-room window – *which had no curtain!* As I remember, my hand travels up to cover my open mouth, an involuntary movement. Alex's body was literally hanging a few inches to the right of that window.

What if Finn had witnessed his father hanging through the window that night? What if *that* was his very last memory of him, dead and pale, with a nylon cord pulled tightly around his neck.

Knowing that Alex hadn't died *inside* the house makes all the difference to how I feel about going home. Now, I actually want to return with the children. I *need* to get back.

Finn, Faye and I pack our bags, hug Penny and Fliss, and we leave.

Thank you.

We wave goodbye through the car windows.

Now, we are three.

I look around at the bare sitting-room walls, which Alex and I had been working on together. They're still dusty, with a single strip of dull green wallpaper left high up on the wall. One corner hangs down, dejected. I reach up and pull it off slowly until it finally pops away from the crumbling plaster wall. These rooms will need to be finished.

Where do I start?

I needn't worry. Stewart arrives the following week with an army of Alex's friends and they get stuck in right away. Every wall is plastered, pink and smooth. New skirting boards are hammered on securely and everything is given a fresh coat of paint. They are my heroes, every one of them. I thank them with mugs of tea and chocolate digestives.

I feel numb.

Finn and Faye go back to school. Their teacher presents them with a book. Every single pupil and teacher has written them a personal message inside it - sweet, kind words of support, brightly coloured letters and pictures. I can feel their sentiment. The net. The safety of their school. Their routine. *My* routine.

This keeps me sane.

We carry on exactly as before. I realise that this is a thing – *before Alex died.*

At night, I hang Finn and Faye's uniforms up on the outside of their wardrobes. I take clean socks and underwear out of their chest of drawers and I go to the kitchen and make each of them a packed lunch – cheese sandwiches for Finn and ham sandwiches for Faye.

Every morning, I reach over to turn my alarm off, long before it goes off.

Alex is dead. This can't change.

I'm weighed down heavily by my thoughts.

I drag my feet to Finn and Faye's room to wake them up. Just for a moment, I wait. I stand in their bedroom doorway, watching them sleeping peacefully.

I envy them.

This silence. Before the noise and chaos of the morning; dressing, breakfast – toast for Finn, cereal for Faye, tea for me. I will eat later. Alone, with the silence of my thoughts for company.

My clothes begin to hang off me. Fear has a way of doing that.

I put our house up for sale because I can't afford to pay the mortgage. Our life insurance must now be null and void because Alex chose to take his own life. *This, our new start.*

No home. No husband. No more Daddy. I'm forty and my life has ended.

Shit. Shit. *Shit.*

How much easier to let go and follow Alex into oblivion.

But I will *never* leave them.

Like Alex left us.

Three weeks after Alex's funeral, Tony, a retired solicitor with a huge fondness for Alex and an even larger dislike for insurance companies, comes to my rescue. Tony is the father of one of Alex's very best friends. He calls and asks me to bring our life insurance documents over to his house. He wants to have a look at them. 'Sure, ok,' I say.

'There's nothing here to say that your life insurance is invalid due to the circumstances of Alex's death, Rachel. Nothing about suicide at all.' Tony squints at the paperwork through his gold-rimmed glasses. We're in his study. It smells of coffee and Pledge. He looks up at me with a serious expression on his face. 'Rachel, you have a solid case here. I'd love to help you fight it.'

So, maybe I won't have to sell our home, after all.

The next morning, I call the estate agent and I ask them to delay putting our house on the market. In the meantime, I arrange to have the interest on our mortgage paid by the state.

For the first time in my life, I'm on benefits.

An idea begins to blossom in the dead days that follow. Day after day after day. Cold breath in winter. Scraping ice off the windscreen. I want to help. I *need* to help people like Alex.

People like me.

CHAPTER 20

Winter turns into spring and gradually it dawns on me that this is for the long haul. The phone stops ringing and friends no longer drop in unannounced. That's actually a relief. The world keeps turning, despite this awful train wreck that has ruined my life.

The rubbish truck passes early, the queue in Sainsbury's, piles of dirty washing – I'm standing behind a thick sheet of glass looking at it all. Watching. I don't belong to any of it. *I'm on the outside.*

Finn and Faye are getting on with their lives. They both seem fine – for now, at least. I take them to school. They laugh. *They sleep.* Sometimes, they ask about Alex and I tell them everything I know – almost. We talk about him over dinner or at bedtime, as if he were a well-loved grandfather who passed away peacefully. That's how it feels, only he didn't.

I take out all of our cards of sympathy and I read them again, one by one. I remind myself. *I go back.*

Because I don't want to go forward.

Today. Today, I'll ring. I've been doing this for days now, telling myself I'll phone the college just outside of town for some more information about a course they're running. I've had their number for weeks. Eventually, when my tea is stone cold, I pick up the phone and, finally, I call. There's only so much of this nothingness I can bear.

'I-I'm interested in your counselling course,' I say with apprehension. I speak to a very helpful and informative receptionist. She has a cheerful, sing-song voice and in less than two minutes, I've booked an appointment to go in and meet the course tutor. Almost immediately, I begin to feel anxious. And there's something else – hope?

Ten months after Alex's death, I'm sitting at an empty desk in a classroom. It's the first day of college and I don't know what to expect. I pick nervously at my fingernails. I cross and uncross my legs. *Is this really what I want?* There's a large clock on the far wall, which tells me it's ten past nine. I'm twenty minutes early. I take a new A4 lined pad and a biro out of my rucksack. I chew the pen lid and look at the clock again.

One by one, other people arrive and sit down at various desks around me. Some also seem to be a little nervous. I nod at them. At twenty past nine, the tutor walks into the room. I sit up. I'm happy to see at least one familiar face, although I hardly know her at all. She puts down her bag, looks across at the clock and says hello to us all. That's how it all begins.

When everything changes.

In between my trips to college, with papers piled high and emails back and forth, words written in just the right way, I receive a letter from the Financial Ombudsman. The life insurance company has agreed to pay out. I read it over and over again. It seems surreal, like a dream — a good one.

I pay the mortgage off and I thank Tony with a case of fine red wine. I write him a letter. Heartfelt words. Because of him, we are able to keep the roof over our heads, for six bottles of wine. Good wine. Of course, it can never be enough. I only hope the letter is.

Somehow, I think that Alex has had a hand in all of this.

Alex.

Suddenly, I am weary. Deep in my bones. I've boxed away Alex's death for several months.

You can let go now.

With the strength of a tsunami, grief comes rushing in from nowhere. I can't stand up. Debris of broken dreams lies all around me, shattered, like glass. I cry until I have no more tears. Only shards. My eyes are swollen and my head throbs constantly. I miss Alex so deeply, sometimes I struggle to breathe.

My grief is raw, like a carcass with no head, hanging upside down. Pink and red. Split open, without entrails.

His smile stays with me. *Huge.*

I look out at the garden and he's playing with Finn and Faye. It's summer and the grass is long and dotted with bright yellow dandelions.

He's laughing.

Blue-grey eyes meet mine.

Fading.

And then I wake up.

I'm crying and my throat hurts.

I roll over and his side of the bed is empty under the flat of my hand.

The sheet is cold.

I can smell him.

I'm at college, one day a week, for the next year and I'm very grateful to have something to break my endless days of going-through-the-motions. Very quickly, I make new friends. We sit in the canteen at lunchtime, eating cold pasta and sandwiches, washed down with lukewarm coffee.

'Shit! Is that the time?' I throw my empty cup towards the large plastic bin in the corner. I miss completely and have to go and pick it up.

We are running back to class, laughing along the hallways like teenagers. *Late.* We talk and talk and talk at lunchtime. Every single one of us has a story to tell — a trauma, a tragedy. In class, we learn how to listen. I feel safe here.

It's almost summer and the course will soon be coming to an end. I want more. I can be real with these people. I can be me *all* of the time. It's addictive being myself.

Now, more than anything, I want to be a counsellor. I accept a place at a different college, a half hours' drive away, which specialises in counselling and psychotherapy. I start immediately after the summer. It will take me at least three years to qualify – two years of college and a further year on placement. But I don't mind that at all. I never look back.

The most significant part of my journey happens outside of college during the weekly therapy sessions, which I'm required to attend as part of the course. At first, I fight it. *Why the hell do I need to be in therapy for the entire duration of the course? A minimum of forty hours a year - how can I afford that when I'm still on benefits?*

Eventually, when I stop resisting, I find a wonderful counsellor called Joan, who charges me next to nothing for the entire time I'm at college. She wears hand-knitted cardigans and thick-lensed glasses. Her eyes are blue and kind and I tell her *everything*. I tell her about Mum, I tell her about Alex and I tell her all about the drugs we took. I feel ashamed telling her that, but she just listens to me and nods. She doesn't judge and I want to tell her more. And more.

Because of my sessions with Joan, I feel a strong urge to write Mum a letter. Eventually, I do. In the letter, I ask her why she was violent and abusive towards me as a child. I describe how it was for me, growing up with her as my mother – how oppressed I felt and how much I hated what she did to me. When I post it, the hurt and fear is back with me like a cloak. I can't shake it off. *What will she say?* This is the very first time I've been brave enough to confront her. I'm forty-two.

I wait. And I wait.

When I finally hear back from my mother, she has photocopied my letter and she's written all over it in red pen.

Lies. Lies. Lies.

Sideways. Right across the black and white pages of my handwritten words. I screw it up, feeling empty. I'm not even angry. I wanted an apology from her, something to say she is sorry after all these years. But… nothing.

I have no mother.

I slam the door shut.

Six months later, I receive another letter. My stomach contracts when I see her familiar scrawl on the envelope and a Barbados stamp with a beautiful blue and green hummingbird. I don't want to open it, nor do I wish to open up old wounds. But eventually, I do.

Mum always writes on yellow lined paper and before I read it, I smooth the creases out with the flat of my hand.

Dear Rachel,
I don't remember any of those things you said about me in your letter. I think I've probably blocked them out but I know you're not a liar.

I want you to know that I always did what I thought was best and sometimes, I got it wrong.
I'm sorry.
Mum
xxx

I'm stunned. This isn't what I expected. I fold the letter neatly and I put it back in the envelope. I'm in entirely new territory here and I need time to let her words sink in. This apology from Mum is unbelievable.

CHAPTER 21

It's October and I only have five months left at college before my final exam, when I hope to qualify as a counsellor. I'm forty-five.

Mike has been staying with me for the last few months. Before that, he was living with Mum in Barbados, although I'm not sure how he managed to do that for so long. He's now in his fifties. Philippa and I think it's probably because he can turn his hearing aid off. *Bliss*, being able to turn Mum's noise off. Not so much the reasons why, though – being deaf. Poor Mike, even he had enough of her in the end. I'm certainly grateful for his company and for his help with the bills.

And then, out of the blue, I receive a message on Facebook Messenger.

Dear Rachel,
I bet this is a surprise! How long has it been? Thirty years? Pedro and I have kept in touch and a few days ago I saw your comment on his Facebook post. I wasn't sure if it was you but then I saw your picture and goodness, you've hardly changed at all!
What are you up to these days? I've been living in England for almost ten years now. I stayed in Bahrain for twenty-five years after you left.

I would love to hear from you!
Frank
x

I read the message again.

Oh. My. God. I can't actually believe it.

I've often thought about Frank over the years. The last I'd heard, Pedro told me he was married with two daughters. As I'm reading his message for a third time, something peculiar begins to happen to my insides. I'm convinced that this is significant and I'm also a little surprised to find I still hold a torch for him after all these years.

I take my time to reply, deliberately holding back. I don't want to tell him everything about me right away. The fact that I'm single, for instance. I keep it brief.

Dear Frank,
Hi. How are you? It's great to hear from you.
I can't believe it's been thirty years since we last saw each other! I only befriended Pedro on Facebook recently and he mentioned that he was still in touch with you. He said that you have two daughters - how old are they?
I have twins! A girl and a boy. They're almost eleven now.
If you fancy a chat, please ring.
Rachel
x

I write my mobile number at the bottom of the message and press send. *Eek!*

A few days later, the phone rings and I recognise Frank's voice immediately. My heart does a somersault, twice. He sounds exactly the same. The years roll back and suddenly I'm sixteen all over again.

Frank and I are on the phone for over an hour, and during our conversation, I finally admit to him that I've been widowed for almost four years. It's not easy for me to say those words; I feel oddly exposed, but Frank immediately replies by telling me he is separated and going through an amicable divorce. Actually, what we're both saying is that we're available, without actually saying those words. I want to see him again. I don't have to wait very long.

We arrange to meet on Guy Fawkes Night in just under a fortnight. Frank lives almost three hours' north of London and I live an hour south of the capital. We both agree, therefore, that London is the most practical meeting place.

I'm excited. And terrified.

Every time I think about him, a kaleidoscope of butterflies takes flight inside my stomach – blue, green, bright orange, purple.

Time slows right down and every day begins to feel like a year.

Finally. Today is the day.

Frank and I arrange to meet under the clock at Waterloo Station at five o'clock. I'm texting him with nervous fingers as my train pulls into Waterloo East. I've just told him I'm a bag of nerves and I think he finds this amusing. I open his text and he has typed three laughing emojis.

At Waterloo East, I make my way over to the main station and walk across the concourse towards the large clock located high up over the central part of the station.

Where is he? I look around but I can't see him anywhere. My heart is in my mouth.

Suddenly, I feel a tap on my shoulder and I swing around to find Frank grinning broadly at me. His face is more mature, but his eyes are exactly as I remember. Kind. Warm.

Chocolate. He's wearing jeans, a pink stripy shirt and a navy blue jumper. He doesn't seem nervous at all. He puts his arms around me and draws me slowly to him. He smells clean. He kisses me full on the mouth. His lips are firm and soft. He tastes sweet. Minty. I kiss him back. My knees have gone.

I've waited thirty years for this.

Without a shadow of a doubt, Frank's kiss is worth the wait. I'm floating.

We walk out of the station holding hands, stealing glances at each other as we make our way along the South Bank, looking for a bar.

Does he like what he sees? This is the fifth outfit I tried on tonight. I eventually settled on dark blue jeans, a long-sleeved white T-shirt and a pink knitted tank top. We match perfectly. I stop short of saying that out loud — that would just be silly — but I think it, all the same.

We pass an array of street entertainers and stop for a while to watch one of them. Frank stands behind me, puts his arms around my waist and pulls me into him. *Can he feel me trembling?* I'm beginning to feel self-conscious, being this close to him, and I'm desperate for something to calm my nerves.

'I need a drink!' I pull away, making light of my nerves.

A little further along the embankment, we find a bar and Frank orders me a large glass of rosé. We sit down together at a quiet table in the corner.

'I've got a little surprise for you in about twenty minutes,' he says, with a twinkle in his eye. He takes a brief look at his watch.

Soon, he's leading me by the hand, back towards the station. At the last minute, he turns towards the London Eye.

'This way,' he says, guiding me through the barriers, into a private pod, where there's a steward and a bottle of chilled champagne waiting for us.

As our pod reaches its highest point, the sun is setting directly behind the Houses of Parliament on the opposite side of the Thames, half hidden behind Big Ben. The entire backdrop is bathed in a golden glow as the glorious expanse of London slowly unfolds below us.

Wow! Is this real? I'm in a dream, sipping chilled champagne on the London Eye with Frank. I keep looking at him. I can't stop smiling.

Much later, I'm on my fourth glass of wine in a bar in Covent Garden and Frank and I are moulded together, holding hands. Now that I've had my kiss, I want more.

'Stay with me tonight,' he says, leaning in as he kisses me on the mouth. 'I've booked a room in town.'

I want to be closer to him. Skin to skin.

'Let me ring Mike…' I whisper, breathlessly. I'm already under his spell.

Mike is babysitting Finn and Faye. He answers the phone sleepily.

'Yeah, sure. See you tomorrow,' is all he says. I have a bus pass.

Within the hour, Frank is letting me into his room. He's booked himself into a budget hotel near Earl's Court. I'm a little disappointed with the drab décor, but I'm also relieved. I'm convinced he'd have booked something a little more swanky if he'd thought I was going to stay in London with him.

Swank or no swank, we tumble into bed, fully dressed. We entwine our limbs around each other like snakes. I want Frank badly and I can already feel how much he wants me. I feel conflicted.

My body is screaming – *Go for it, Rach.*

My mind is saying – *Not on your first date, Rachel.*

Stuff you, mind, says my body. And then we're naked. Joined. It's a night for first kisses and for making glorious love in a rather shabby hotel room. I couldn't care less.

I've had the best night of my life.

I'm staring up the yellowing artex ceiling as Frank begins to snore loudly next to me.

Ok, so this isn't at all glamorous, but inside, I'm flying like an eagle, high up over the rooftops of London... over the Houses of Parliament, the London Eye and Tower Bridge. Golden lights shine in the windows far below — white stars, pinpricks in the night sky above.

I wouldn't be sleeping, even if I could.

After our first date, Frank and I spend the next few weeks travelling the almost two hundred miles between us so we can be together whenever time permits. We're restricted by Frank's work. He's often abroad, but he's as keen as me to spend as much time as we can together. I'm reassured by that.

When Frank comes to stay for the first time, he appears very relaxed. He already knows Mike from Bahrain and they greet each other like old friends. Finn and Faye seem excited to have someone new in the house to talk to and Frank is easy and natural with them.

'Do you like Thai food?' he asks.

Finn almost immediately screws his face up. 'Is it like curry? I don't like curry,' he says, matter-of-factly.

'They've never tried it. I've only tried it once and it tasted like washing up liquid to me,' I reply, sticking my tongue out and opening my eyes wide. Frank laughs at that.

'I'd love to make you all my Thai green chicken curry,' he persists. 'My girls love it. Maybe you will, too?' He tilts his head to one side, encouragingly.

'I'll try it,' Faye says, sweetly, never one to let anyone down.

'Me too,' Mike pipes up from the sofa. Mike eats everything.

Frank's cooking is the perfect icebreaker. Finn, Faye and me chat together in the kitchen while Frank cooks. They both interact with him as if they've known him for some time.

'These are hot. I like hot food,' Faye says to Frank, waving a green chilli. It's true. Unlike Finn, she likes spicy meals.

I haven't yet met Frank's two daughters, Sienna and Harper. They're both away at vocational boarding schools but will be staying with Frank over the Christmas holidays. Frank has invited me over for New Year's Eve so I can meet them both. *Eek!* I hope they like me.

It's two days after Boxing Day and Frank and I are driving over to pick Sienna and Harper up from their mother's. We pull up outside the house and I flash Frank an anxious look.

'I'll stay in the car,' I say, cowardly.

'Ok.' He nods, smiling, as he reaches over to squeeze my thigh before climbing out of the car.

A few minutes later, both girls begin chatting away happily from the back seat, as if meeting me is an everyday occurrence. I'm relieved.

We spend the next few days cooking, going for walks and playing video games together. Sienna borrows Faye's walking boots, which I keep in the boot of my car, crusted with mud. They're a little too small for Sienna and end up giving her a large blister, which makes me feel very guilty. Sienna is a dancer and her feet are very important. She reassures me that she'll be ok.

Frank, Sienna and Harper are especially amused at my lack of skills on Mario Kart, much to my chagrin.

'Shit. Oops, sorry,' I apologise, as I crash for the umpteenth time.

'You really are crap at this,' Frank shouts, as he overtakes me, unscrupulously. I stick my tongue out at him and sit back down on the sofa, pretending to sulk. Sienna and Harper laugh at me. This feels like Christmas.

Soon, I'm saying goodbye to the three of them and driving back home. I hope I've made a good impression, because I really like Frank's girls.

And I really like Frank.

Spring arrives and so does the day of my final counselling exam. I'm sick to my stomach with nerves as I pull into the car park. It's taken several years for me to get to this point and I simply can't afford to fail. Quite literally. I need to start earning, and soon.

However, I needn't have worried. In less than two hours, I'm back in my car with the biggest smile on my face.
I've passed!

I drive away from college for the very last time, on an all-time high.

When I arrive home, I immediately call Frank and give him the good news. He's almost as pleased as me when he finds out. So is Penny, who I call next. She offers to take me out for an early dinner to celebrate with all of the children and, happily, I accept.

However, it doesn't take long for my bubble to burst.

We're all sitting around the table, eating in the nearby gastropub, when Penny's daughter Fliss, pipes up with a comment that shocks me.

'Why were you talking to Rachel's boyfriend on social media last night, Mum?' she says, innocently. My pulse begins to race and, almost immediately, I can feel adrenaline coursing through my veins. Penny does her very best to brush it off, but suddenly, after years of lying dormant, the tar-black monster is roused. I'd almost forgotten he existed.

I'm trying to eat, but I don't feel like putting anything else in my mouth. Mostly, I'm scared. Penny has been single for a while now and that worries me, because I know she and Frank have recently become friends on social media. Until that moment, I hadn't realised that they were communicating with each other. *Privately*.

Penny suddenly seems very uncomfortable. She won't look at me directly anymore. Fliss looks nervously between the two of us, and because I've experienced such a strong physical reaction to her words, I don't trust myself to speak or to press Penny for an answer. The tar-black monster stretches out his twisted limbs. I can smell his rancid breath as he yawns, showing his huge jaws and a flash of yellowing teeth. The entire evening has been completely ruined, on the day I've finally qualified. I should be celebrating.

Instead, the atmosphere in the pub has changed. I feel miserable and I can't wait to leave. I don't have the courage to tell Penny what's going on inside my head, because I don't know whether I need to be concerned or not. Try as I might, I just can't shake the feeling that something isn't right.

Several days pass and I've been tormenting myself. I've returned to the days when my mind used to play terrible tricks on me, back when I was smoking cannabis… although I haven't touched it in *years*.

I know it's risky, but the situation has been eating me up from the inside and I need to get it off my chest, once and for all. I sit down at my computer and I write Penny an email because

I'm not feeling brave enough to ring her. I ask her outright if anything is going on between her and Frank. I feel a little ridiculous when I see my words typed out on the screen in front of me, but I hit send before I talk myself out of it. I only wish I'd had the courage to speak to Penny when it actually happened.

Only a short while later, Penny rings me. She sounds shocked that I'm questioning her loyalty and flatly denies that there is anything going on between her and Frank.

I immediately feel ashamed for doubting her and more than a little embarrassed that I'm showing myself up. However, part of me also knows that I need to be absolutely straight with Penny if I'm ever going to get past my fear. It's something I learned during my counselling course – address the elephant in the room. *My elephant.* The fact remains that Penny was communicating with Frank privately and, however innocently, I suppose I'm walking headlong into a lose-lose situation – either I hurt Penny's feelings for doubting her or I lose her friendship for calling her out. The latter is the tar-black monster's take on the situation… the tar-black monster who also happens to be *me.*

The following day, when Frank and I are alone together, I muster up the courage to speak to him.

'Frank, I really need to talk to you about something,' I say, quietly.

'Sure, what's up, Rach?' he says, looking up from his iPad. I now have his attention. I take a long, deep breath.

'I'm scared. I-I'm frightened I'm going to lose you. I mean, I've got this huge irrational fear, which is all-consuming sometimes, about loss in general. Well, not just about loss, but also that you might be unfaithful to me.' I've now shrunk to the size of a small child. At least, that's how I feel. Despite this, I continue, before I lose the courage to finish what I want to say. I explain everything that happened in the pub with Penny and I also tell Frank about the email I sent her the previous day. It's the first time I've ever been totally honest with anyone about my insecurities, because I feel so utterly ashamed about it.

'Rach, I'm really sorry you feel like that. Yes, I did communicate with Penny, but it was perfectly innocent, I promise you. Just banter.' He moves to sit next to me, picks up my hand and squeezes it gently. I want to cry. 'Rach, you lost Alex in such a horrible, tragic way. I'm not the least bit surprised you've got a fear of loss.' His voice is low, almost a whisper. I'm desperately holding back the tears. I swallow hard.

'I know. But I felt the same way with Alex. I think it's always been there, hiding in the background. When I started smoking cannabis, well, I didn't know what was real or not and it really affected my trust... my ability to trust. *Anyone.* And I want to trust you. And Penny. I really do. I just don't know how to do that right now.' And then the tears spill over and I can't stop crying. Frank is holding me and we stay like that for a while, until I'm calm and my head hurts.

From then on, Frank is very patient with me whenever I feel insecure, although I struggle to tell him every single time that I'm feeling worried or anxious, because it happens so often. I'm ashamed when I feel unsure of myself and I'm terrified when I think that my fears might be founded. Sometimes, when Frank is away, terrible scenes play out inside my head. I imagine him meeting Penny in New York when he's there for work:

She arrives at his hotel and walks up to the reception desk, wheeling her Delsey case behind her. She checks in, collects the key and turns around to walk across the stone floor towards the lift, her heels echoing on the tiles. When the lift door slides open, she steps inside. Minutes later, she is walking out of the lift onto one of the upper floors, leaving behind a trail of Issey Miyake. She walks up to Frank's empty room, her footsteps silent on the plush carpet. She inserts her card and lets herself in. She undresses and covers her nakedness with a white towelling robe from the back of the bathroom door. She positions herself on the bed and waits. Soon after, Frank enters the room, still in his uniform. It turns her on. They make love and after they make love, they talk. She asks about me, almost casually. But this dark act, this betrayal, is how she lives and breathes. This is her power, this clandestine affair. She beguiles him, saying all the right things to make him hard. To make him love her. He crumbles because he is weak.

All of this takes seconds, this film reel inside my head. It plays, over and over. Sometimes, the scenes change:

She is sitting at the table of a restaurant, leaning in towards Frank, provocatively. She takes an ice cube out of her glass with red-painted fingernails and she sucks on it, looking directly into his eyes. Her eyes say, "Fuck me, Frank."

It wrenches at my insides and in the pit of my stomach, the thought of this terrible betrayal. My best friend and my lover. Together. Conspiring. She loathes me. *I can actually feel it.*

Stop it, Rachel!

I wish I could, but I can't. I just can't. The tar-black monster is playing these clips, over and over inside my head. Sneering. Taunting me.

"You stupid bitch," he says. *"I own you."* And he does.

When Frank returns home, I say, 'Have you been behaving yourself?' But I never tell him exactly what I'm thinking, about the sordid scenes that flash through my mind. I'm too ashamed.

Sometimes, when it's really bad, I imagine Frank repeats some of the things I say to her. I hear her words, her nuances, in his language, and his in hers. Cruel coincidences. Corroboration, inside my muddle of a head.

'There's nothing going on between me and Penny. Or anyone else, Rach,' Frank assures me, quietly. And yet, despite Frank's patience and understanding, the tar-black monster continues to raise its ugly head. *My* ugly head.

Please. Go away!

Almost inevitably, Penny withdraws from me.

Does she know?

Very soon, she stops communicating with me altogether. I message her a few times over the following weeks and months. But she isn't interested in anything I have to say. As far as she's concerned, I've burned my bridges.

I feel terrible about what's happened to our friendship of over thirty-five years. I also feel responsible, *mostly*. But there's no going back.

After hearing what's happened between Penny and me, Connie also takes a step back. She declines every single invitation to meet me and Frank until it becomes embarrassing. Eventually, I give up and retreat with my tail between my legs. I probably deserve it... all of it. After all, I didn't trust Connie when Alex was alive, either. I had a whole set of show reels for her, too.

There's a common denominator in all of this mistrust and it's me — my pathological fear. It seems almost ironic that I've manifested the very thing that I've been most afraid of – losing the people I love the most. I'm terrified I might do the same with Frank.

CHAPTER 22

Exactly ten months after our first date in London, I ask Frank to move in with me. I want him close.

'I'd love that,' he says, simply.

When the dust has settled and the loft is filled with boxes of Frank's belongings, yet to be unpacked, the house feels different... a kind of prosthetic limb to replace the one I ripped off. *I will learn how to use it. I will teach myself how it works.*

I'm grateful that Faye accepts Frank from the very beginning.

'Where is Frank?' she asks, sweetly, whenever he's gone.

'He's gone to work, darling,' I say.

'Oh,' she says, disappointed. She notices his absence immediately.

Finn, however, is very different. When Frank is at home, he flies off the handle for no apparent reason. But of course, there *is* a reason and I blame myself. I never allowed Finn or Faye the opportunity to fully express their own grief, because I hid mine away. I wore a mask for so long. It's taken me years to understand this. *Six years.* Frank's presence highlights Alex's absence in ways I hadn't yet considered. This new prosthetic limb of mine.

It's Saturday morning rugby in the fog and I'm shouting the loudest. I'm the only mum on the sidelines today.

'You're embarrassing me,' Finn says. His hair and clothes are caked with mud. I'm thinking, *I'll be washing those later.*

On another occasion, we're in the park and a boy on his bike says 'Daddy,' looking up at his father. Finn throws me a look. He is glaring at me as if this is my fault. I imagine words forming inside his head. He's saying to me, *'Where's mine?'*

That word, *'Daddy.'*

He's gone.

Is it me? Am I projecting this?

I'm too frightened to ask Finn what it's like for him and so, selfishly, I avoid these conversations. I brush him off because I'm scared it will open me up, talking about Alex.

Old wounds.

Not old enough.

Gradually, I allow myself to believe that Frank is with us for the long haul. Crucially, I begin to believe that he genuinely wants to be with us, although it's not always plain sailing. Like a canal boat, we have to negotiate our way through many a lock before we can move forward. Often, Frank and I are forced into our adult skin. We have to take a breath and work things out. I'm just relieved that he *wants* to work things out — all the niggly, not-so-nice things that come with the reality of living together. Finn watches all of this unfolding with suspicious eyes, silently observing us while eating his toast.

Often, one of us erupts… or more than one of us, if it's a real humdinger. It starts from nowhere. Silence, then almighty hell breaks loose and we revert to using some pretty colourful language. At! The! Top! Of! Our! Voices! Stuff the neighbours.

Normality. I slowly begin to see normality in all the chaos of our family life and I realise that it's ok for us to disagree, argue or shout about the things we feel strongly about. This doesn't mean that Frank will walk out or do something violent.

It's safe. We always make up afterwards.

I'm the most stubborn – the most wounded. I've been living on my nerves ever since the day that Alex died. Six years is a long time to feel scared. Fear has been the driving force for most of my life and I've been frightened for as long as I can remember. Fear of abandonment. Fear of loss. Fear of loneliness. Fear of failure.

When I allow myself to stop and just *be* with Frank, when I allow myself to trust him, there's no place for any of my fears to take root. Fundamentally, I know that I can count on Frank and I like that feeling. I like the security of it. He's my invisible net. He's *there*. It's impossible for me to feel scared when I let go. But letting go is so frightening and the responsibility on me is huge. Ultimately, it's me in the driving seat, and this makes me feel vulnerable and exposed. It terrifies me.

It's time for me to let go of the tar-black monster. I've been running away from him for most of my life. I've been running away from *me* for most of my life. It's time to stop running. And I do.

Over the next few years, some of the best times I have with Frank are during the summer holidays when we take all four children away. I love it most when the six of us are all together: Sienna, Harper, Finn, Faye, Frank and me.

For our first summer together, we visit Frank's mother and stepfather in France. The following year, we take two weeks off and we drive down to Cornwall. Philippa has offered us the use of her house for the first week, in exchange for dog-sitting duties. After that, we'll be moving to a rented cottage nearby, meaning that we can spend some time with Philippa and her family when they're back.

'Let's take Suzi to Tremayne Quay,' I say to Frank, a few days in. Suzi is Philippa's Springer Spaniel. We normally take her down to the beach, but today, I fancy something a bit different.

'Sure,' Frank says.

This is the first time during the holiday that Frank and I have been alone. I take his hand as Suzi bounds down the stone path. Almost immediately, she darts to the right, disappearing into the lush green undergrowth. Like a periscope, she pops her head up through the foliage to look for us and then she's gone again. This makes both of us laugh.

Frank and I walk under the dense canopy of ancient trees, their branches thick with moss and lichen. The emerald-green of felted limbs. Stone-grey fossils on trunks of gnarled bark, like huge, powdery snowflakes. Whispers. Cool air. Shadows. We fall into silence. Rustling leaves. Sunlight, like spattered paint on a woodland canvas.

There is magic here.

At the very end of the path, the foliage gives way to the solid grey walls of the quay. A sudden expanse of sky appears above me. I blink. Ahead, the river flows sideways. Choppy. Directly opposite, I can see a mirror of ancient woodland behind the riverbank on the opposite side of the estuary, with a gentle breeze on my cheek. There's the slightest scent of ocean. Suzi is still, sniffing the air, motionless except for the slight twitching of her nose.

We turn, to retrace our steps. This time, Frank takes my hand. I look at him. *There.* Something *is* different. *Does he feel it, too?* Suddenly, he seems serious… sad, almost.

'Rachel?' His voice trails away. My heart stops.

'What? Yes? Frank. *What?*' I say, swallowing hard. I stop walking. Frank turns to face me, his eyes shining.

'Rachel, will you marry me?'

I stare back at him, blankly. I'm not expecting this. I struggle to take in his words. I'm expanding. I feel the roots beneath me in the cool earth, a mesh of sinew. The trees surrounding us. They are watching, I'm certain of it. Wispy clouds, soft and pale, drift overhead. *This moment.*

'Yes, Frank. *Yes.*' I say. I want to be with Frank forever.

Driving back, an idea comes to me.

'Frank, let's have an engagement party. When Philippa and Patrick are back.' We've already arranged a family barbecue at the cottage for the following week. 'It's the perfect time to announce it, don't you think?'

'Good idea. It'll be even more special.' Frank smiles broadly.

I arrange for my father to join us. He suffers with dementia and now lives in a care home, near to Philippa.

'I'm busting him out for the day,' I joke. Dad can only get about in a wheelchair these days and so I arrange for a specially adapted taxi to collect him.

Several family members turn up: my half-brothers Ray and Mike, Frank's cousins and also Frank's mother, who is over from France, staying with us.

The day is warm and bright. It's a perfect summer day. We are all outside, some standing and some sitting at the patio table. Dad's wheelchair is pulled up at one end. He's hunched over slightly, but his eyes are sharp, taking it all in. Frank's cousin is turning sausages over on the barbecue. There's the gentle hum of friendly conversation. Laughter. A rumble over what music to play next. *It's definitely a Bob Marley day,* I think, with a smile.

Frank and I nod to each other and we duck inside to retrieve several bottles of chilled champagne from the back of the fridge. I return with a tray of champagne flutes and plastic tumblers for the children. Frank clears his throat. My heart is beating fast. It's time.

'Can I have everyone's attention for a minute?' Frank raises his voice so he can be heard above the music. Someone turns Bob off. It's silent.

Frank turns around to look for me and I step forward, suddenly self-conscious in front of all these familiar faces.

'Last week, Rachel and I went for a walk down to Tremayne Quay, and while we were there, I asked if she would be my wife.' He pauses, serious for a moment. 'I'm pleased to announce that she said "Yes".' He grins and there's a wave of noise — cheers and a high-pitched whoop. Frank's cousin slaps him on the back.

'A toast,' Frank says, 'to love.'

'To love,' we all say, raising our glasses. The champagne is really rather good.

Dad is sitting in his wheelchair under a large umbrella, out of the summer sunshine. He raises his glass to us with a wobbly hand and spills a little on his lap. I'm so happy he's here with us today.

In less than two months' time, he'll be dead. His heart will stop beating over breakfast as he's eating his bacon and eggs in the dining hall of his care home, perched high up on the cliff with a spectacular view of the rugged Cornish coastline.

What a way to go.

CHAPTER 23

Dad's funeral is a happy affair, just a handful of us seeing him off in a quiet Cornish crematorium. The service is both solemn and uplifting. Right out of the pages of a 1950's Vogue magazine, my aunt stands up and walks to the front of the small whitewashed chapel.

She is poised. Commanding. Her voice is clear and steady. She remembers my father with her words. Beautiful words. Her brother. Our Dad. She shares a few of our precious memories. She depicts his love, particularly his love of women. This makes us all laugh. Just behind her and a little to the right is Dad's coffin, dark wood with brass handles. *My father is dead.* In reality, he left us years ago. Today is almost a relief.

As we leave the chapel, Philippa approaches Dad's coffin. She places her hand on it. Her mouth forms silent words, words that are only for him. They had something special, those two.

I watch her leave and, suddenly, I'm self-conscious. I walk up to Dad's coffin and I stop. I linger, running my fingertips lightly over the polished wood… the briefest touch. *I cannot wake you. Or laugh with you at the silly things.*

Bye, Dad.

Thank you.

Dad's death makes me think about my mother in Barbados. I haven't seen her in ten years and the last correspondence I received from her was her apology. I'd like to see her, at least one last time, and so I mention it to Frank later that day.

'Frank, I think I should go and see my mother. You know, before it's too late. I was thinking maybe you and I could make a holiday of it at the same time.' I'm trying to convince myself more than him.

'I'd really like that, Rach. Leave it with me.'

That's how it always is with Frank. He just gets on with it and is happy to do whatever I ask. Before long, he's booked us a week away at an all-inclusive resort in Barbados, near Speightstown. I ask Mike to look after Finn and Faye for the week, as usual.

Frank and I are unpacking in our hotel room. It always amazes me how quickly he organises himself. Every time we go away, he unpacks his entire suitcase before anything else. He hangs up his shirts, puts his smalls away in a drawer and empties the contents of his washbag on one side of the bathroom sink, neatly arranging his toothpaste, toothbrush and any bottles. I suppose it comes from a lifetime of travelling.

He's landed.

Eventually, I do the same, but only because I feel slovenly if I live out of my suitcase.

It's our first evening in Barbados and we're freshly showered and have changed into lightweight clothes, more suitable for the tropics. Almost immediately, I feel an overwhelming desire for an ice-cold rum punch. It's only four in the afternoon but I don't care. We're on holiday! I begin to feel excited.

Our hotel is located high up on a ridge with a constant easterly breeze to keep us cool. We make our way down to the poolside bar together and order a drink.

'Cheers,' Frank says, smiling.

'Cheers,' I reply, touching my glass lightly against his before taking a sip. There it is, the tang of lime and dark rum – rich, oaky and sweet caramelised sugar with a dusting of nutmeg.

'Wonderful,' I say, breathing in the view. Our hotel looks out over the west coast and, although the sun is still high in the sky, in less than two hours it will be setting directly in front of us. *I've really missed this.*

My mother has no idea I'm on the island. I'm going to surprise her, but first, I want Frank and I to have a couple of days alone together in this gorgeous hotel where everything is included. I feel a little guilty for not rushing over to her apartment immediately, but I'm also very wary after what happened on my last trip with Alex. I want things to be completely different this time and, for once, I know exactly what to do.

Frank and I have seven days on the island. Once my mother knows I'm here, she's going to want to see me all the time. However, *I'm* going to call the shots this time. *I'm* going to make all the decisions.

'As long as she knows she's going to see me regularly, she'll be fine,' I say to Frank, hopefully. 'I'd like you and me to have a couple of days together first and then we can surprise her. I'll need to schedule a few things in the diary with her and pepper them throughout the week so we can still have some time together. *Alone.*'

Frank leans forward and kisses me full on the mouth. 'I'm happy to play it any way you want, Rach,' he says, looking at me with soft brown eyes. Eyes I want to fall into. He opens his arms to me and I step into his embrace. I press against him and I feel his desire. I kiss him again. Tease him.

'Let's go,' I say, through lowered lashes.

I want you.

This man who has stolen my heart. This man who loves me.

I've wanted you for years.

Suddenly, I'm back in Bahrain. *Reeling.* I'm sixteen again, waiting for Frank to arrive at the Dilmun Club, knowing nothing of love. I want to see him. Be close to him. Lie naked with him. When he finally walks in, my heart does a somersault. It's such a powerful feeling. *Desire.* This is what I'm feeling now. Desire for Frank, all these years later.

Only this time, I can have you.

And I do.

Frank and I park our small hire car and walk up to my mother's brightly painted single-storey apartment building. It's turquoise, with white contrasting burglar bars on the louvred windows. I haven't been here before.

Frank takes his phone out. He wants to capture the moment. He stands back as I knock on the door. To add to the deception, I call out in a broad Bajan accent.

'Hello?' I say through the open louvred window to the right of the front door.

'Who is it?' My mother's voice, familiar but somehow different. Older.

'Hello?' I repeat. A giggle is bubbling up inside of me. I throw Frank a look. My co-conspirator. He's grinning back at me, videoing. He nods towards the door as my mother opens it.

'Oh my God. My God,' she says, looking at me. 'Rachel...' her voice trails off.

'Give me a hug, Mum,' I say. She looks old. She *is* old. We hug each other. She's eight inches shorter than me and she's lost weight, a lot of weight. I'm looking at a thin, frail old woman. She's sunken. Bowed. My mother is a shadow of her former self. She invites us both in and I introduce her to Frank.

Mum chatters away non-stop. I hear her words. Pleasantries. 'When did you arrive?' 'How long are you here?' Underneath, I'm doing my very best to stay here. *Her voice*. It pulls me back. I'm a child. I'm frightened. *I hate her.*

No.

I blink. She's talking to Frank. She's asking him about work, on the charm offensive. I'm struggling not to see my abuser. This woman persecuted me. Beat me. Bit me.

Stop.

I can't stay long. I'm hot and claustrophobic. Adrenaline is coursing through my veins and I want to run. I don't want to sit and discuss how comfortable our hotel room is.

Eventually, I'm unable to take it anymore. I already have an itinerary for our remaining five days on the island. I've planned it military style to prevent any unwelcome visits. Today is Monday. I tell Mum I will see her three more times:

On Wednesday, I'll return on my own. Mum offers to make me lunch, which means I'll probably have to stay longer. *Shit.*

On Thursday, Mum will come to our hotel for lunch.

On Friday, my brother Casper, and his family will bring Mum to meet Frank and me at a different hotel near Speightstown. It's the same hotel where Connie, Penny and I climbed aboard a white-and-yellow speedboat to take me to Alex on our wedding day. *I wonder how that will feel?* It was Casper's suggestion, as Mum likes it there.

On Saturday, she can come to the airport to say goodbye. *If we make it that far.* I know how much she likes an airport goodbye.

She seems happy with my timetable and so Frank and I leave.

'You ok?' he asks, once we're in the car. 'You went very quiet in there.'

'I was really struggling,' I say. Frank knows everything about my childhood and the abuse. He doesn't speak again and nor do I, not until we're back at the hotel.

'I need a rum,' I say, as soon as I've taken the key out of the ignition.

'Fine idea, Rach.' He smiles.

On Wednesday, I'm back on my mother's doorstep, with the same old rubbish washing over me. It's tiresome, all this rubbish. I've had enough of it.

'Can I offer you anything? Tea?' she asks. 'I only have condensed milk.'

I want to say, 'How about a different childhood?' or 'A mother who cared about me?' or even 'A mother who isn't batshit crazy?' But I don't say any of that. Instead, I say, 'Tea is fine, Mum. Condensed milk is fine. Thank you.'

Mum invites me to sit down with her at the dining table. It's painted white, like much of the wooden furniture in her small sitting room. The chairs have brightly coloured cushions – a tropical pattern in blue and yellow – colours of the Barbados flag. One of the cushion ties is missing and when I sit on it, I slip and have to steady myself, not just physically. My nerves are all over the place.

Today, I'm going to speak to Mum about my letter. I'm also going to speak to her about all the abuse and the violence. I haven't mentioned her letter of apology, although it's the main reason why I'm here in Barbados. I want to have it out with her, face to face, and put everything behind me, once and for all. I need to do this, for me.

I launch right in.

'Mum, I was really upset when you wrote back to me saying I was a liar about all of the things you did to us – *to me* – when I was little.' I don't recognise my voice. It sounds strange. 'I was ready to write you off. That was *it*, as far as I was concerned. It really was.' I look up at her directly, non-threateningly. Truthful. At least she has the decency to look down at her tea, this saggy old woman in her sarong. *Something.* I feel a whisper of something in my core. It's out of reach… within me, but much too deep to access it.

She brings her mug up to her lips and blows gently, almost absent-mindedly, with glazed eyes. She's gone somewhere. She returns her mug to the table without taking a sip. She sits up in her chair and shifts a bit.

'Rachel. I'm so sorry. So much about those years, I erased. I blotted them out. I know I hit you. And your Dad. I feel terrible about that. I feel terrible that your Dad is gone and we didn't speak for years.' She looks younger, briefly. I catch a fleeting moment, a memory of them together. 'I miss him,' she says, unhappily. She's old again. Weary. 'When I was still a child, my mother left us. Left Jamaica to go and live in America. You already know that much. My sister Patricia, went to live with my aunt, but my brother John, and I stayed with my father. Dad was a tyrant. A monster.' She takes a deep breath and continues. 'He was furious that my mother left him. He would beat John and me all the time. He beat me black and blue – said he was beating the Boújais out of me.' I recognise my grandmother's surname. I'm horrified.

'Rachel, I know it's no justification for what I did to you children, and to your Dad. But I was angry about everything…' her voice is quiet now. 'I'm sorry,' she says, simply. Truthfully. Without defences up. Just her. *Her story.*

Suddenly, I recognise this wisp of a feeling within me and I want to put my arm around her and say it's ok. I want to tell her I understand – that I know how she feels. And, of course, this is why she's telling me – because she knows already. This woman. My abuser. The irony of it.

At that moment, I could so easily have stood up abruptly and walked out without saying another word, without seeing her again, *ever*. I could have slipped down inside my pain, crushed by the weight of it. I've carried it around my entire life, *because of her*.

But I don't.

Instead, I sip my tea, and Mum gets up and walks over to the hob. She lifts the lid of a large stainless-steel saucepan, releasing a cloud of steam, and stirs the contents. I've seen her doing this a thousand times.

But everything feels different. *I* feel different.

Frank and I enjoy our remaining few days together, including the times we meet again with Mum. She's back to her chatty self, talking mostly to Frank about her past. Stories she thinks will impress him. He winks at me when she's not looking. Frank already knows everything about her. She'd be horrified if she knew just how much.

This time, when we say goodbye at the airport, I feel ok. Everything feels just right.

'See you again, soon,' I say, giving her a big squeeze.

My frail, old Mum.

And I mean it.

CHAPTER 24

I wake up on Easter Sunday in Philippa's spare room. I'm fifty. I've slept heavily and I'm feeling a little disorientated. My eyes adjust and, as the fading images in my dreams give way to reality, I remember.

Particles of dust float in a thin shaft of sunlight, illuminating the narrow gap in the heavy-set curtains. I get up and open them wide, filling the room with bright sunshine. I'm looking through the window at a clear blue sky. I touch the glass. It's cool beneath my fingers. I breathe the air deep into my lungs, holding it there for just a moment before exhaling slowly through pursed lips, in a silent whistle.

Today is finally here.

Philippa has created a makeshift dressing area for me and my seven bridesmaids in her converted barn, only a stone's throw from the main house.

The hairdresser arrives early with her baby bump and a case full of paraphernalia. We sit, looking in the mirror at ourselves and at the ornate frame surrounding our reflection. We talk to each other through it, chatting to the hairdresser as she works with her nimble fingers. One by one, we are tonged, plaited and fixed with a fine mist of spray, which makes me cough.

I am briefly distracted by the sound of tyres crunching noisily on the gravel outside – a delivery. Two large cardboard boxes of flowers; pink peonies and white ranunculus, bound tightly together. Eight bouquets. Philippa takes the boxes and puts them carefully down on the side. I watch her peek inside and smile.

On the far wall of the barn, on a makeshift rail, a row of dresses. *Waiting*. I walk past with rollers in my hair, my hand trailing lightly over the fabric inventory: a subtle shimmer of silvery grey dresses – *six*; feather stoles in white – *eight*. My fingers sink into them, curling into their softness. At the very end of the rail, ivory gowns – *two*. The smaller one is for my goddaughter, Lulu. My little one, not yet ten. And finally, mine, heavy and full. This finery, for my entourage. My support. I look around for each of them. Philippa's daughters Tamsin and Lola, are applying their makeup. Casper's daughter Bella, is having her hair plaited. Faye is talking to Philippa. Sienna is pulling faces and making Lulu laugh, and Harper is watching them, smiling.

This moment.

Laughter and the warmth of family, all around me. The sunlight beating bright, warming the flagstones outside. Reaching through the large glass windows into the barn. Casting golden shapes on the wooden floor. Rectangular highlights.

Suzi, Philippa's elderly spaniel, stumbles in, grey-muzzled and wobbling on her unsteady legs. She doesn't see so well these days. Her snout meets the edge of my chair. She stops, resets her course and steers right, towards the kitchenette. Philippa and Patrick float through the melée with glasses of chilled champagne.

Soon, we are ready. We fall in, standing together on the gravel drive in a perfect line, clutching our bouquets for photographs.

The barn is now empty of us. We leave behind a scent of perfume and hairspray. A smudge of red lipstick, lightly imprinted on a champagne flute. An open palette of eye shadow. A single feather stirring lightly on the wooden floor. Drifting.

Moments later, a 1960's bus pulls up on the road outside to collect us – dark green with chrome bumpers, adorned with ribbons and flowers. It has a name – *Hughy*. My heart is beating rapidly. *Thump, thump, thump.* I climb in, using both hands to lift the heavy folds of ivory fabric in my dress. I find the narrow steps with my shoes and I climb, gingerly. One. Two. Three. I shift sideways through the doorway. Inside, I twist around to find the edge of the red leather seat behind me. I step backwards and I sit, awkward with the fullness of my gown. Faye walks past, down into the belly of bus. She smiles at me, my beautiful girl. One by one, we fill the bus with our dresses and flowers... and our voices.

Hughy pulls away, bouncing, as if in slow motion, on old suspension that creaks. It makes us laugh. A waft of diesel and then we settle into our journey. The air outside flows through the open gaps in the windows, through glass panels, slid sideways. Stuck with age. It keeps us cool. A shaft of sunlight flashes through the trees as we pass. Pink cherry blossom. Then, white. A moment of calm as the breeze stirs tendrils of hair around my face. I take the stillness and I draw it into me, gazing out of the window. A clear expanse of blue beyond the leaves. Behind me, a rising tide of excitement. Everything is exactly as it should be.

We pull up outside the stone walls of the castle, perched high up on the hill, overlooking Falmouth and the bay, far below us.

This is it.

We spill out of the bus and slowly make our way over a large expanse of grass to the small stone keep. Finn is standing outside waiting for me. This is the first time I've seen him wearing his suit – a traditional kilt of Cornish tartan, black and yellow, with a thin strip of turquoise and white. He runs up to me and throws his arms around me. I feel crisp, starched fabric against the softness of my stole. I hold him close, this handsome boy of mine. He seems older somehow. We pass under the heavy stone archway, thick with white roses. Their sweet, familiar scent.

I take a deep breath and step into the subdued light of the entrance vestibule where we gather together, my entourage and me. My heart beats rapidly inside my chest.

At the far end of the room, I peek around the doorway, stealing a brief glance inside the keep. I watch them. *I listen.* The hum of family and friends on benches in neat rows. The backs of them. Bright splashes of colour. Hats. A glittering hairpin.

At the end of each row, on either side of the aisle, a single church candle encased in glass, neatly placed in the centre of a wooden barrel, surrounded by a garland of fresh white roses. Wooden hearts, strung cheerfully on wooden pillars lining my way.

To Frank.

Where he stands alone. Those broad shoulders I know so well.

Waiting.

Suddenly, the keep falls silent and Lulu looks at me with her bright blue eyes. I smile back at her and nod. She takes her place in front of me and holds her bouquet aloft, clutching it with both hands, her grip steady and strong. Faye steps forward and brings my veil carefully over my head. Our eyes meet briefly before I'm hidden. They're Alex's eyes. Behind me, in pairs – Tamsin and Lola, then Faye and Bella, and finally, Sienna and Harper.

Finn appears next to me – he is giving me away. His edges are blurred through the ivory haze of my veil. I'm trembling slightly as I slip my hand into the crook of his arm. We've practised this. A rustle of fabric. A shuffle of grit under my shoe on the wooden floor. And then silence. It's time.

The music begins and Lulu steps forward. We make our way through the doorway into the back of the circular candlelit keep. Step by step, we walk together, in perfect unison. Slowly, past the barrels with candles, flickering. Casting shadows on the rows of faces, eyes reflecting the golden light. The glint of a watch. A cough. Anticipation poised, curled tightly between my ribs.

I look up and I see him. My heart skips a beat as he looks at me with shining eyes. His love, I can feel it.

This man who found me. This man. *Frank.*

Photo by Alan Law

ABOUT CHERISH EDITIONS

Cherish Editions is a bespoke self-publishing service for authors of mental health, wellbeing and inspirational books.

As a division of Trigger Publishing, the UK's leading independent mental health and wellbeing publisher, we are experienced in creating and selling positive, responsible, important and inspirational books, which work to de-stigmatise the issues around mental health and improve the mental health and wellbeing of those who read our titles.

Founded by Adam Shaw, a mental health advocate, author and philanthropist, and leading psychologist Lauren Callaghan, Cherish Editions aims to publish books that provide advice, support and inspiration. We nurture our authors so that their stories can unfurl on the page, helping them to share their uplifting and moving tales.

Cherish Editions is unique in that a percentage of the profits from the sale of our books goes directly to leading mental health charity Shaw Mind, to deliver its vision to provide support for those experiencing mental ill health.

Find out more about Cherish Editions by visiting cherisheditions. com or by joining us on:

Twitter @cherisheditions
Facebook @cherisheditions
Instagram @cherisheditions
Cherish Logo

Cherish
EDITIONS

ABOUT SHAW MIND

A proportion of profits from the sale of all Cherish books go to their sister charity, Shaw Mind, also founded by Adam Shaw and Lauren Callaghan. The charity aims to ensure that everyone has access to mental health resources whenever they need them.

You can find out more about the work Shaw Mind do by visiting their website: shawmind.org or joining them on

Twitter @Shaw_Mind
Facebook @shawmindUK
Instagram @Shaw_Mind

Your Local Mental Health & Wellbeing Charity